SHATTERED

From Grief to Joy

after My Son's Suicide

Rebecca Tervo

DISCLAIMER: I take full responsibility for my thoughts and feelings and beliefs. In telling this story, I realize that many times I blamed others for what I was feeling and thinking. Looking back with better vision and lots of self-help, I now realize that I had way more responsibility than I took at the time. I felt it was necessary to lay out what my grief experience was in MY perception in order to take you through how it felt to lose Trevor to suicide. It was not my intention to hurt anyone during the telling of this story.

**IF YOU OR SOMEONE YOU KNOW IS IN CRISIS
CALL 9-1-1
OR THE NATIONAL SUICIDE PREVENTION
LIFELINE AT:
1-800-273-8255**

To Trevor—

I wish I'd have known the pain you were in, so I could've tried to help.
You are always in my heart.

Trevor, Christmas 2015

I Am

I am a thinker who loves books.
I wonder why we are part of the universe.
I hear a life calling, for I have yet to get one.
I see my future, but I can't reach it.
I want to be a better person.
I am a thinker who loves books.

I sometimes pretend that I'm a sane person.
I feel another's pain when they suffer.
I touch my dreams, but can't hold on.
I worry about my family and friends.
I cry when I chop onions.
I am a thinker who loves books.

I understand that some things are worth fighting for.
I say anything is possible.
I dream to make life easier for mankind.
I try to make a difference.
I hope that I can help the world in my lifetime.
I am a thinker who loves books.

—*Trevor Tervo*
written during middle school

TABLE OF CONTENTS

INTRODUCTION

EARLY 2012—MY comfortable routine of going to work, coming home, eating supper with my husband and four children, and participating in the kids' school and sports activities unexpectedly got thrown out the window hurled into an abyss, and landed in a shattered heap.

That shattered heap—that was me, my new life scattered at the bottom of a deep, dark pit.

It's difficult to account for the chaos my world became, but I'll do my best.

My days were fuzzy and full of physical and emotional exhaustion. My nights were long and sleepless.

"How can I possibly go on living like this?" the broken-record voice in my head called out, leading me to tears, confusion, and greater fuzziness.

Food appeared in the refrigerator though I couldn't bring myself to go to the grocery store. Church was the last place I wanted to go as I felt all eyes were on me judging me for my parenting skills.

Some days, I felt strapped to the La-Z-Boy, physically unable to answer the door, my body unable to respond.

I tried to absorb the kind words of others written in cards and sent over with food dishes, but from the bottom of the abyss, it was just so difficult to receive any communication. When friends called to find out how I was doing, the conversations seemed to make little sense to me. I had a hard time concentrating on what they were saying. If someone offered to help, I had no idea what they could help with. Again, I was living in a foreign territory, and these friends appeared as curious reminders of the place and life I had come from.

My formerly highly organized life was in shambles. My emotions swung wildly between anger and impatience to tears and depression.

Apparently my husband lay at the bottom of his own abyss. We could almost hear one another and almost interact with our children, our community, each other. Almost.

Sometimes I'd hear him say, "We're doing fine, as well as can be expected," a response I found confusing. I certainly didn't feel fine.

I don't remember much about how, or if I did any parenting at all during those months. I later realized that our daughter Kendra, who was in seventh grade, was taking on the mothering role for our second grader, Annika.

I was mentally and emotionally absent from the life my husband and I had built with our children over the past 20 years.

You see, during the early morning hours on Sunday, January 29, 2012, our 17-year-old son, Trevor, took his own life in his bedroom using my husband's handgun while the rest of us were fast asleep.

2017—Why am I still here when my son is not? I figured there must be a reason that I experienced this devastating loss in my life.

In seeking answers about why I was still here, I pieced myself together and raised myself out of that lonely hole. I began clawing my way back to "normal" from the incredible grief and despair and hopelessness. When I was able to have more and more "normal" days, I started to work on finding clarity in my life.

By using specific practices and tactics, I've now come to a place of peace and acceptance. I'm now reconstructed and back on the surface—not the same as before—but more alive, aware, compassionate, and appreciative.

I reconnected with my husband and our children. I have a renewed relationship with God. I am sleeping through the night.

I am taking care of my mental and physical health (I've even lost over 20 pounds!). And I've changed careers and started doing what means most to me right now—coaching women to help them overcome obstacles, set exciting goals, and achieve those goals to realize their most fulfilling life.

This new life feels amazing and wonderful. I am in awe of where I was before and where I am now—and I can't wait to share my journey with other women who are struggling to find meaning in their lives.

"Am I living a life on and with purpose? Am I living the authentic life that I am here to live?" This book gives the story of how I moved from no to yes in regard to these questions.

It will teach you how to ask yourself these questions with compassion and fearlessness, and it will give you practices, examples, and inspiration, so you can find your way to yes too.

Before proceeding, let me share that on the 5-year anniversary of Trevor's death, I posted a personal video clip on Facebook in which I shared how hopeful and inspired I now feel about my future and the future of my family. That video has now been viewed almost 2,000 times. Here's the link to it: www.rebeccatervo.com/index.php/book-additions

I encourage you to take a moment and watch that short video and then return to the book. It will give you a shot of inspiration as we start together on this courageous journey of choosing to live an authentic, purpose-filled life.

1.

BEHIND THE DOOR

I REMEMBERED HAVING a strange dream, one that I hadn't had for a while since my youngest child was already 8 years old at that time. You know when you have a dream that seems so realistic that it startles you awake and makes your heart beat a bit faster because you're thinking it's true? It was that sort of dream.

The dream was that my husband, Rob, and I had been in the hospital, and I had given birth to another baby—a baby boy. This would be our fifth child as we already had two girls and two boys. It was quite a shock to me, and in those initial moments of waking up I was worried about how I was going to keep my job, the job I had just taken about six months earlier as the business manager at the Northern Michigan University (NMU) Foundation. I had always stayed home for one to three years after each of my babies was born.

When I realized the dream was just a dream, I kind of laughed and gave a sigh of relief. Later this dream came to have significant meaning to both of us.

As Rob was awake too, I relayed the dream to him. He kind of joked that it would be OK with him.

As is usual for us on Sunday mornings, Rob and I woke slowly, lazily getting out of bed and deciding who would drive our girls to Sunday school that day.

It was a normal Sunday morning, January 29, 2012.

I emerged from our bedroom and went to my daughters' room to get them up, so we wouldn't be late for Sunday school.

Beep . . . beep . . . beep . . . beep . . .

In my daughters' room I could hear a phone alarm sounding. I realized our son Trevor must have left his phone in the chair of the upstairs family room that was between his room and ours. So, I dug the phone out of the chair and slid it under his door, so he would wake up.

I went downstairs to prepare breakfast and see that the girls were getting ready for Sunday school.

Beep . . . beep . . . beep . . . beep . . .

Even still, the alarm continued to sound in the background.

Knock, knock, knock.

"Trevor, will you please get up and turn off that alarm? It's been beeping for five minutes now," I heard Rob say to Trevor through his door.

KNOCK, KNOCK, KNOCK.

"Trevor! Turn that thing off and get up!" Rob hollered.

I was sitting at the table downstairs, eating scrambled eggs. I could hear Rob getting annoyed upstairs.

Beep . . . beep . . . beep . . . beep . . .

Because the alarm continued to sound and Trevor wasn't answering Rob, I knew the scrambling I was hearing from upstairs was Rob trying to get the door open himself. He was trying the penny trick, the one where you can open an inside-locked door with a penny, but apparently that wasn't working.

Beep . . . beep . . . beep . . . beep . . .

The house we were living in was an old house built in the late 1800s, and we had done a whole remodel job on it. Some of the doors, like Trevor's, were still those old cheap hollow bedroom doors that were easily pounded through—and that's what I heard next—Rob bashing through the thin door.

Next, above the beeping sound of the alarm, I heard a sound so bizarre that it's difficult to describe. The best I can do is compare it to the noise an animal that is in unbearable physical pain might make. Though it didn't sound human, I knew it came from Rob.

My daughters heard it too.

We raced up the stairs to Trevor's room.

Rob had slammed the battered door shut and was standing against it on the inside. We couldn't get in.

Bam, bam, bam, bam, bam. I pounded frantically and started crying in terror.

I felt out of control. Desperate.

"What's going on? Why won't he let me into Trevor's room?" raced through my mind.

I started to feel that there must be something bad behind that door, but my mind couldn't come up with a possibility.

What was behind that door? What did Rob endure alone and refuse to allow me to see?

Looking back, I am so thankful Rob didn't let me in that room.

Our dear 17-year-old son Trevor was lying on the floor in a pool of blood from a gunshot wound.

The rest of the day was a blur. The police and an ambulance arrived. The girls and I stayed out of the way.

The police had a question for me, but I honestly can't remember what it was.

I do remember totally falling into my husband's arms with the policeman standing next to us and me, crying out, "How does a mother *not* know her son is depressed?" I couldn't figure out any reason that our talented, smart, 17-year-old son would take his life. We had much to learn about teen depression and suicide, a world we'd never wanted to be flung into.

As the police finished their investigation, they found a note in Trevor's pocket and handed it to Rob. They asked if this was Trevor's handwriting. Trevor had a very sort of messy, childlike style of printing even at 17. I found it cute and charming. It was easy to see that the note was written in Trevor's handwriting.

When Rob confirmed it, the police let us read the note. I don't remember much about what the note said. I do remember it giving a message that we not blame ourselves and that Trevor loved his family and friends very much.

It was all too much to handle.

I had the girls come with me to the downstairs bathroom, so we didn't have to witness the black body bag being carried out to the ambulance. It was unbearable.

Rob insisted that he clean that room all by himself that day. He cleaned away the blood and scrubbed the floor. He made the room sparkle, as if nothing had happened in it.

In perfect contrast to the room, I went from organized to confused that day. And that's how I stayed for a very long time.

2.
FUZZY BRAIN

WHO WAS RESPONSIBLE for my son being dead?

Questions, racing thoughts of what had happened. Even wild stories about some conspiracy or something that was going on.

Saturday, January 28—Had something bad happened that day that had made Trevor want to kill himself? What was going on?

That Saturday there had been a bowling meet in Manistique, a town about 2.5 hours away. Trevor was on the high school bowling team, a conglomeration of students from Ishpeming and Negaunee High Schools. The team was extremely successful as they had been to the state championships several years in a row already.

That Saturday Kendra, our daughter in the seventh grade, had a swim meet with the YMCA swim team, so I was in Iron Mountain at the meet with her all day. Rob and our other daughter Annika had stayed home as Rob was helping a friend move.

It seemed like a normal Saturday.

The last time any of us talked to Trevor was that Saturday night around midnight. He still wasn't home from the bowling meet. Rob had texted to ask, "You doing OK?" Trevor replied, "Yep," a total Trevor response. Trevor was still at the bowling alley in Ishpeming, bowling some final rounds.

As Trevor was a different sort of kid, unique, something I'll talk about later, I remember being happy for him that he felt a sense of community and friendship with the bowling team.

I still remember that he was the last one to leave the bowling alley that night. Kendra had been downstairs playing the piano when Trevor came into the house that night. She said he didn't say anything to her, just bounded up the stairs as if headed for bed.

A few days after that Sunday the bowling team came to our house to spend time with us.

The team was in shock. They had all spent that Saturday with Trevor and were combing their memories to find anything that would give them a clue about what he had planned.

Thankfully one of the girls had taken some pictures of him that day. The one that I will cherish forever is one where he has a huge smile on his face and is wearing his favorite Beatles t-shirt. When I look at the picture, I don't see any sign of a troubled soul.

The coach told us that Trevor had sat with him on the bus returning from the meet. They had talked about going to states again, and Trevor seemed happy with that. The coach confided that he remembered thinking, "I'm so happy to see Trevor coming out of his shell."

Trevor had always been an introvert. He took pleasure from doing things alone, things like reading, building large Lego structures, writing poetry, playing the guitar, writing and illustrating comic book stories, and teaching himself how to play the piano.

Later we would read that a suicide victim often appears to be happiest after they've made the decision to take their life.

Many friends and family came and sat with us. They sang songs, but all I kept thinking was "I don't want any reminders of Trevor. I don't want to look at any pictures of him. I never want to go into his bedroom again to see the emptiness there. Never."

I told my sister-in-law that day, "I just want to throw all the pictures away."

Bless her soul, she replied, "You might want to wait and be patient before taking any actions. You've got time."

I felt like everyone was looking at me to see how I was feeling.

While I've never been a drinker of alcohol, I was feeling a pleasant kind of buzz that I imagine is similar to a tipsy state. While my body was sitting in that room surrounded by friends and family, inside myself I was far away. My brain was fuzzy, and I felt like I had entered an alternate universe that was far from reality.

There were practical things that had to be done—funeral arrangements. Who wants to go pick out a casket for their child? My parents came to help.

It was the weirdest time. I remember telling my husband, "I don't care," many times when he'd try to get me in on a conversation about the cemetery plot, the casket, the service, etc.

I just wanted it taken care of and over with.

Over the days until the funeral, we had many visitors—school friends, neighbors, teachers.

One of the teachers that came to visit was Trevor's favorite teacher, his poetry teacher. The poetry teacher had told us at parent teacher conferences in October 2011 that we should ask Trevor to share his poems with us. She relayed that he was an amazing writer.

When we had asked Trevor to see his poems, he'd sort of brushed it off but had come home with a poem titled "Sand." It was a beautiful poem.

After that Sunday Rob called the school and asked if they could bring all of Trevor's poetry to us, so we could read it. We knew Trevor had poetry, but other than "Sand" he hadn't really shared any of it with us.

While the poetry teacher was visiting, she shared that Trevor had written some dark poems, but she hadn't been able to find all of them at school, even after looking in his locker. We didn't really think anything of it but read all of the poems she offered. Some were so deep. Especially in my stage of shock and grief, I couldn't understand what they meant. But, reading the words that I knew my son had written was somewhat comforting at a time when I was grasping for anything to lessen the unbearable pain.

Weeks later, Rob got the courage to start processing the stuff in Trevor's room. It was only then that he found the "dark poems" that the teacher had been looking for. Trevor had neatly folded them up and placed them on the top of his garbage can as if to leave them as a clue for us.

One of the poems talked about how depressed he was and ended with "Perhaps I'll find solace in the grave: my new home." There were several others that seemed to us to have incredibly dark meanings, enough that we wondered why the teacher hadn't told us or anyone else about the poems. It was obvious she'd read them since they were graded with As and had comments like "Nice job" written on them.

This was one of the hardest things for my husband and me to let go of.

3.
THE FORMULA FOR RAISING KIDS

NOW, BEFORE YOU wonder what had gone on in Trevor's life to "make him" kill himself, I want to assure you that I've reviewed our life with a fine-tooth comb over and over again, trying to figure out where we went wrong.

You see—as far as I was concerned, we were "normal."

Rob and I had both graduated from Michigan Technological University. We got married the summer before our senior year in college. Rob graduated as an engineer and I as an accountant.

We started our family immediately and ended up having two boys and two girls over the span of 11 years. We did what we were "supposed" to do. Rob worked as an engineer, and I stayed home off and on with the babies between part-time jobs.

For the first 4.5 years after college we lived in Dixon, Illinois. However, once we decided we wanted our kids to go to a small, safer school than what we felt was available in Dixon, we moved back "home" to Upper Michigan where I was raised and sent our kids to the school district where my mom was a teacher. It felt like we were doing what we needed to do to have a "regular" family life.

We took the kids on a big trip at least once a year. We had taken them to Disney World, Mississippi, Tennessee, and Florida several times. We took them camping in the summer. We encouraged them to participate in sports that they enjoyed during the school year. We lived close to our church, and we made sure they went to Sunday school and learned about God.

I was a mom who wanted my kids to have friends, so I was more of the planner that tried to have them invite friends regularly. I also wanted them to be well-rounded, and if I noticed something they had an interest in, I'd try to find a program they could be a part of.

With Trevor, it was a variety of things. He was the type of kid that seemed to want to know about everything. His interests ranged from wanting to write comic books (I remember finding scraps and papers of drawings of comic book characters over the years) to getting a telescope, to wanting a microscope, to spending one summer hunting for treasure with his metal detector, to getting a magic set and learning all the tricks, to building Legos, to liking those fantasy board games.

He seemed especially interested in music, so I started him in orchestra in the fifth grade playing the cello. I even sent him to orchestra camp one summer in our area. He took an interest in bowling, so I signed him up several summers in a row for free bowling summer sessions. After the cello, he'd play the harmonica, guitar, piano, and ocarina.

Later, he would have an interest in golf, but he would get really frustrated with it since he couldn't control that dang ball. One of the funniest stories was when Trevor, in exasperation, laid himself right down in the grass on the golf course on one of the final days for the junior golf league and said something like "I guess I'm just not old enough for this game." His perfectionistic ways didn't work well with golf, but he did still end up on the high school golf team for a couple years.

I could tell that he was a kid that needed to be constantly challenged. Some of his elementary teachers said they had to keep things for him to do separately from the class because he was on a different level and was often bored with what they were learning. By the sixth grade, he was at a twelfth grade reading level.

Many times I've wondered what would've happened if we'd moved somewhere so Trevor could've gone to a more specialized school that would have encouraged his gifts and talents.

The only concern Rob and I sometimes had was that Trevor didn't have much of a social life outside of going to bowling meets and golf practices. We wondered where his friends were and would ask sometimes. Sometimes he'd get a small group together to come over and act silly, and then I'd feel better again that he had friends. But we wonder sometimes if that was something we should've been more concerned about. He seemed to like spending time alone and that felt OK to me. I thought, "Boys don't need best friends like girls do."

Who really knows the answers to all these questions? I've thought about them and talked about them over and over.

I still can't figure out what would've been the big thing that would've told me that my son was suffering from depression. Yes, after reading his poems, I could see the depression—but before that, nothing.

We really had no answers. Even now, we think we know some things that we've pieced together in the years that followed, but really, we have had to conclude that we just didn't know what we didn't know.

It's hard, especially as I'd thought that if I did this, this, and this, then I would get this certain result with my kids.

Turns out I had no control over my kids' lives all along. I was just kidding myself that I had any control over who they were going to be and what choices they'd make and what kinds of mental and physical illnesses they'd face. From the perspective of a control freak and perfectionist like me, it was a hard realization to come to terms with and one that turned my life upside down. This was a huge part of my grieving process.

There were unending questions, something we were told by our different counselors was normal. My brain just couldn't figure out the enormity of what had happened, so it would continue spinning on the same questions over and over trying to find a solution. For me, I couldn't bear to face the fact that everything I'd thought about how life worked was wrong.

In fact, I have a very logical, step-by-step brain (something Trevor definitely got from me) where if you do A, B, and C, then you get D. I had figured that raising children worked like this:

A. You marry a man who has similar moral and religious values as you.

B. You have children together and bring them to Sunday school and church every weekend.

C. You read bedtime stories in the younger years to get them interested in reading and books.

D. You spend family time together on the weekends and supper at the same table every evening.

E. You take the kids on vacation every year to a warmer spot on Easter break, so they can explore different areas of the country.

F. You take the kids camping in the summer to let them enjoy the outdoors and woods and campfires and swimming.

G. You encourage them to explore their interests and put them in things like the summer bowling program, junior golf program, and summer day camps. You even encourage them to start playing an orchestra instrument in the fifth grade and pay for them to go to the summer orchestra weeklong sleepover camp.

H. You attend every single one of their parent-teacher conferences to find out how they are doing in school and make sure you are helping them if there are any difficulties.

I. You hug them lots and tell them you love them.

J. You visit grandparents and other family regularly to give them a sense of their bigger picture background.

K. You infuse their life with music, all kinds of music from pop to country to classical (I love music☺, and I'd like to think Trevor got his love for music from me).

L. You encourage them that they can be anything they want when they grow up, and you try to have conversations about that as they get older (Trevor wanted to be an inventor at one point and at another time wanted to write comic books).

M. You buy them things for Christmas that feed their imaginations. Trevor was so into Legos, telescopes, microscopes, magic sets, metal detectors, guitars, and ocarinas. We realized the pattern in the last years of his life: he was totally into learning about something and using it to its full extent while he was learning it. Once he figured it out, it was on to learning about something else. He had this unending thirst to learn new things.

N. You guard their young minds against violent TV, movies, and video games.

O. You discourage using bad language and swearing.

P. You try to feed them healthy, home-cooked meals as much as possible.

That's what I thought the formula was for raising a family and having the kids go off and be happy and successful in life. Therefore, I just couldn't understand where we went wrong.

My brain would review over and over snippets of our life— family vacations, lovely Christmases, game nights, birthday parties, camping trips. It just didn't make any sense to me.

What had we missed?

4.
BABY STEPS

TREVOR'S BEDROOM WAS a scary place to me for a long time. I remember at the beginning avoiding even looking in that direction. It was difficult because the door from the master bedroom opened up to face the opposite end of the living area where his door was. Sometimes I'd close my eyes until I got to the top of the stairs; other times I'd turn my head to the left and focus on the stairway instead of the bedroom door.

I knew I'd eventually have to go into his room, so I started with baby steps. I'd walk to the door, then turn around, and decide I'd try again later. Eventually I got to the point where I'd start to open the door. The overwhelm and fear of completely opening the door was so great that I'd quickly close it again and decide to try on a different day.

One day I opened the door and stood just inside the doorway. The crushing pain that came from being in the room was so overwhelming that I rushed for his bed where his stuffed gorilla sat. I hugged the gorilla and sobbed so hard I thought I'd never stop.

I had many crying sessions lying on his bed like that. It was a deep crying from somewhere inside that was hidden so far away.

I honestly thought my crying sounded like it was coming from a different person—that's how primal, profound, and wrenching those releases were. And after I'd finally let up, my face and eyes felt so swollen I thought maybe I needed an ice pack.

In some ways I felt this fathomless crying might make things better, but in other ways I wondered when it would end. I didn't know if it was healthy that I'd started associating going into his room and lying on his bed with this deep, deep sorrow.

Eventually, I started rifling through his stuff: reading the little notes he had collected and pinned to the bulletin board above his desk, looking through his dresser drawers, sorting through the music and books he kept on his shelf.

I felt unsettled about the fact that he had pinned different clippings of colleges he was thinking about attending. One of them was a music college that I had never heard of.

Trevor had talked about being an inventor or a comic book author in years past, but I couldn't remember the last time I'd heard him talk about his future. Looking at those clippings it seemed like he had been making plans about his future. There was also a note that was tracking his volunteer hours for the National Honor Society.

Just these little things were devastating to me. How could he just "quit" in the middle of his life?

His life was just about to begin—and he knew it too.

It just seemed so pointless.

We were building a new house and planning to move out and sell this one. I couldn't bear to live in the house where my son had died. No one offered to help clean out his room—and I'm not sure I remember asking anyone to help—so I did it myself.

Rob had already done the hard stuff, cleaning up the blood and disarray from the night Trevor died.

I tried not to feel sorry for myself that I had to do the other cleaning alone.

I went through his clothes and kept his favorite t-shirts. Trevor loved to wear t-shirts with things on them. His very favorite was the Beatles t-shirt. But I remembered another one he wore often that was red with an owl on the front. Dylan, our other son, has several of Trevor's t-shirts that he still wears. The other clothes went to my nephews, just in case they could use them. The dresser now lives at my brother Scott's house.

It's so hard to let go of Trevor's things. We still have his Lego Knights' Kingdom Castle that's fully built with the little knights and horses. We have his keyboard, his ocarinas, his guitar, his yearbooks, and his favorite music CDs. We have his mindbender games, his metal detector, his telescope, and his whole Garfield book collection. Anything personal to him, we still have it. I don't really know what we'll do with it all. At this moment, it's earned a closet in the basement.

I am sometimes so amazed that God let me be the mom to such a brilliant, quirky, humorous kid. He was so fascinated with how things worked, he was so cuddly and huggable, and he was always fair to a T about everything. If there was a dessert to be split between all of us, it was usually Trevor that waited until everyone had taken a piece, so he'd take the last one. If there was something to split between him and Dylan, he'd let Dylan choose first. He was incredibly fair to the penny in money situations. In his brain, I could sense there were no gray areas, only black and white.

I loved his quirkiness. He had such a deep understanding of the English language and had apparently read the dictionary cover to cover at least twice, according to one of his friends. He used big words that I hadn't heard of, sometimes as early as the sixth grade. He had a fascinating brain that had a thirst for knowledge. He had such intention about learning everything he could.

We have told people that he read more books in his young life than many adults will ever read in their entire lives. His nose was stuck in a book most times. When we'd go to see Dylan's basketball games during his middle school years, Trevor would come along with his book and never see a minute of the game. Same with college hockey games. He'd come, but we always joked that we had to pay $10 to have Trevor sit and read his book the entire game.

In school, Trevor's head was off in the clouds lots of times. He was a bright student who was ahead in reading comprehension, and I often wondered if he was too bored to pay attention. He already seemed to know so much. There are lots of those kinds of questions. If we had challenged him more academically, would it have kept him alive? Or would he have been depressed no matter what we did?

Trevor was goofy and fun-loving too. One time, I took Dylan and Trevor to Disney's Animal Kingdom by myself on a trip to Florida. Rob stayed back at the condo with the girls who just wanted to have a pool day. So, off the three of us went. We were determined to ride Expedition Everest, the largest, scariest-looking roller coaster there. This one went through the dark, went backwards, and had a big monster Yeti that frightened you at several spots. We ended up riding that coaster at the end of the day and went on it twice in a row. But, Trevor wasn't done—he went on it all by himself several more times until the park closed. He couldn't get enough of the thrill.

At that same park, they have an attraction called "A Bug's Life" based on the movie. I thought, "How bad can this be?—it's based on a kid's movie, right?" It's a 4D movie theater that felt so realistic. I had Dylan on one side of me and Trevor on the other. I was freaked out right from the beginning, and the spiders coming from the ceiling had to be one of the worst parts. I screamed louder than almost anyone in the huge theater. Trevor and Dylan were just laughing at me. Trevor was like "Mom, this isn't real!" They had more fun laughing at my reaction, and none of it seemed to faze them.

I remember fondly all the experiences I've had over the years with Trevor at theme parks. I'm so thankful we got to spend those precious times with him when he was so enthusiastic about experiencing new thrills. Oftentimes I could see his mind working, trying to figure out how the rides got put together.

Trevor certainly wasn't your average student. Like I said before, he was amazingly bright and devoured books to gain as much knowledge as he could. He was always on top of his homework and never needed or wanted any help with it. He was determined to make it on his own in life.

Did Trevor feel alone? Did he feel unloved or ostracized? According to the school notes from the kids, it seemed that bullying happened during middle school. In high school, it appeared that many people were in awe of how great a poet Trevor was and what a great sense of humor he had. I believe he found his place in high school. And, even found a group of friends to hang out with on a regular basis. Maybe I was kidding myself—but his life seemed full of robotics, friends, music, bowling, golf, and downhill skiing.

Christmas seems lonely now. Trevor was such a delight to shop for at Christmas. He was so over-the-top appreciative of gifts that I couldn't wait to see his reactions. I remember one Christmas when he had asked for the large set of Knights' Kingdom Legos. I found them on a good sale and was so excited to purchase them that year. We were in the middle of a remodel of a 4-square house we were turning back into a single-family home. We were living upstairs while we worked on the downstairs. I found the perfect hiding spot in an out-of-the-way closet downstairs.

Christmas morning came, and all the presents were opened. I realized as I was cleaning up the kitchen that I hadn't seen Trevor open the Lego set, and it came to me that I had forgotten to look in that downstairs closet! Quickly improvising, I got the gift and came into the living room to announce that Santa had dropped a gift in the back stairwell, and it was for Trevor.

Trevor had this look of wonderment on his face. He grabbed the gift and opened it and was in such a state of elation it was hard to keep up with everything he said. One thing that struck me was "Holy cow—this was $100 at Target, wasn't it? WOW!!!!" And he proceeded to clear everything off the table and get right to work. He had the whole large castle and all the vehicles and people built within several hours. And then he continued to play with it the rest of the day.

That Lego set sat on a shelf in his bedroom until the day he died. It was a sad reminder to me of what a fun kid he was at Christmastime.

These are the things that are hard to let go of.

5.

MISSTEPS, MISUNDERSTANDINGS, AND MIXED MESSAGES

Note to the reader: Rob made contributions to this chapter

SOME ASPECTS OF the school response to Trevor's death were hard for us to understand.

The kids on the bowling team were mostly from a neighboring school, as it was a combined bowling team between the two schools. These kids told us they weren't allowed to wear specific t-shirts or anything to honor Trevor. However, when a revered football and track star that had graduated from that neighboring school died by suicide six months later it seemed to be treated very differently. There were all sorts of school and community activities surrounding his death including memorial type things that had not been allowed for Trevor.

That outpouring prompted some of those bowling team members to question why they weren't allowed to do anything in school to honor Trevor's memory.

We didn't understand it either.

Trevor's school seemed not to allow anything in the yearbook regarding Trevor. One of the most painful things was that his picture was not included with his class in the junior yearbook. Not a single word was mentioned either—it's as if he never existed at all.

There was also nothing the next year in the senior yearbook. In years past, I'd seen a page of a senior yearbook dedicated to a classmate that had died, whether from cancer or a car accident. But not for someone that dies by a mental illness. NOPE, they are stigmatized.

The class president did mention him in her speech at graduation and offered a moment of silence which was really nice. According to his friends, other little things had been planned, but most not allowed by the school.

Someone who dies suddenly from an unknown heart condition is celebrated in a way. They are revered. However, someone who dies suddenly from an unknown brain condition is often pushed under the rug in what could seem like an attempt to forget them. Like they never existed.

That's one of the worst parts for parents of a child who died by suicide. It almost feels like you aren't supposed to talk about them. You aren't supposed to have questions for the school and the teachers who interacted with them every day. When you go to the guidance office to question some things that happened in poetry class, you are sort of assured that the school is addressing depression and suicide, so everything is now OK.

One of those things we were concerned about was a movie, *Dead Poet's Society*, that was shown in class only a few weeks before Trevor died. In this film, Robin Williams (how ironic that he also later died of suicide) plays the role of a teacher in a boys' school. During the film, one of the boys, Neil, ends his life after having an argument with his father. He kills himself exactly the way Trevor did: at night using his father's gun while his parents are sleeping.

When we watched the movie later we couldn't help but notice that it contains no message of hope for the surviving students in Neil's class. The message in the movie is quite disturbing. It leaves the suicide as an unanswered dramatic statement of a way out for a young person who is struggling with some perceived conflict or challenge in their life. Nothing is said after the suicide to convey a message to the viewer that there is hope for life, that every life is precious and worth living, that there is help available for depression and suicidal thoughts, and that suicide is not the solution.

In *The Mystical Gaze Of The Cinema: The Films of Peter Weir,* Richard Leonard writes that Peter Weir, the director for *Dead Poet's Society,* was worried about a copycat situation with this movie. So much that he tried to make Neil's character appear weak so the suicide wouldn't be perceived as a noble act. He has received criticism for not making Neil appear weak enough.

Trevor had seen this movie that seemed to romanticize suicide. Afterwards there was no class discussion that offered alternatives or critiqued the message of the movie, and there was no suicide prevention education accompanying the showing of the film. We found it unconscionable. I talked to the guidance counselor about that very concern, but it was brushed off like it was normal. I beg to differ. Kids need a better message.

Essentially the message we were getting at the time was—let's not talk about Trevor's death. Let's not look at what was missed or what could have been done differently.

We found it ironic that there was much concern given to preventing friends from memorializing Trevor. His picture was left out of the yearbook due to an apparent concern of copycat suicide. However, so little concern was given about showing a suicide movie without any depression awareness or suicide prevention education to go along with it. It just didn't seem to make sense.

Before going any further, let me say emphatically, it wasn't anyone's fault!!

We know the reason Trevor died is simply because he had the brain disease of depression. We didn't know he had it, but he did. Nothing that anyone did or didn't do, said or failed to notice caused Trevor to die by suicide. Bottom line, it wasn't anyone's fault that he died by suicide. We believe this with all our heart.

That fact doesn't mean we shouldn't try to learn everything that we can from Trevor's suicide so that others may be helped before it's too late. Our hope is others can be guided to the help that they need to recover from depression and live long, healthy and happy lives. That's our vision for Trevor's legacy.

Kids need to know to alert a trusted adult if they hear their friend say something that they feel could be a cry for help. Adults need to know the most effective way to respond when such information is brought to them. We all need to learn about the signs of severe depression, even the less obvious ones, so we will recognize them when we see them and be empowered to take action to save a life.

Since Trevor died, we have heard of several kids who have alerted adults and parents about their friends who have shown a need for help. Some of them have told us that they wouldn't have been concerned if they hadn't known of Trevor. I often wonder if the reason he had to die this way was to shed light on the topic.

We are extremely happy that Negaunee High School now offers QPR training to all high school students and school staff. QPR stands for *question, persuade, refer*. It is a one hour training designed to teach people the warning signs of a suicidal crisis and how to respond. In fact, since Trevor died, Negaunee Schools has become one of the more proactive schools in our area for depression awareness and suicide prevention education.

During all these trials we were facing, questions about what really happened, Rob's obsession with trying to figure it all out and solve this unsolvable riddle, I was not doing too well. I began self-medicating with sugar. I figured, "Why should I care about what I eat?" At one point I thought it would be better to get cancer and die, so I could go be with Trevor.

It's at this point that I'll describe my journey through grief and despair in more detail.

6.
PLANET GRIEF

I THOUGHT I had been through grief before. In fact, I had.
My baby brother, Darin, was 19 years old when he died of osteogenic sarcoma (bone cancer) in 1997. I was 27 at the time. My husband and I had our boys by then. Dylan was 4 and Trevor was 2 at the time. We have this amazing photograph of my brother Darin with Dylan and Trevor on the day of Super Bowl XXXII when the Green Bay Packers played the New England Patriots.

I always thought it was interesting that the Packers were in that Super Bowl at that time, the first time in 30 years (and they won it 35–21), because it was in time for Darin, a huge Packers fan, to participate in it before he died later that year.

In the photo Dylan and Trevor are wearing adorable little Packers sweaters. (Rob, Dylan, and I are Packer Backers, but Trevor wasn't so much a football fan.) I often think now how it's nice that Trevor and Darin are together in heaven.

The difference between the grief I felt when Trevor died and the grief I felt when Darin died was on different planets: (a) Trevor was my child and Darin my brother; (b) Trevor's death was so sudden and Darin's was like a long, slow four-year good-bye. We knew Darin would eventually die of the cancer even though there was hope in those first few years that he could beat it. Trevor's death was so shockingly sudden that there was no way we would've had time to prepare for it.

When Darin died, I grieved for the future without a sibling group of five. He was the baby of all of us, and I was the oldest. I just couldn't imagine why he'd been taken before he got to experience the fullness of life: having a girlfriend, graduating from college, getting married, and having children. I just knew he would've been a great dad.

At the time, I had two preschoolers and a newish job at an accounting firm as an auditor. I was very busy and had to take care of my family. The grief went on for a while but was nowhere as intense or persistent as what I experienced from losing Trevor.

It was difficult and lonely during those first several years after Trevor died, and food became a constant companion. I used it to try and stuff the feelings down. The feelings of shame over what Trevor had done. Guilt for missing something that I should've seen as his mother. Anger at what the school was not doing and hadn't done. Anger at friends, family, coworkers, and acquaintances for not saying the right things. To be honest, I wonder sometimes what anyone could've done or said that would've made me feel better. I doubt there was anything. All I knew was that I had gone from being so optimistic about life and feeling so blessed to falling into a deep, dark pit of despair and grief.

I learned a lot about grief through my own experience of it after Trevor's death. First, I was surprised by its physical manifestations. I was extremely exhausted. I felt like I had lead blocks weighing me down all the time. But, I couldn't sleep. Each time I'd close my eyes to try to sleep, my mind would start the thinking and problem-solving process: "What if we'd done this? What if someone had heard him say that? What if we had asked more questions? What if the teacher had done her job right? What if, what if, what if . . . ?" It was exhausting.

Beyond the exhaustion, there was the physical tingling and numbness. I figured it had something to do with what I was going through, but it was really annoying. I'd just be sitting down to coffee with a friend and suddenly this wave of tingles/numbness would ripple through my body. I could feel it down to my fingertips and all the way down to my toes. It was freaky. I'd even tell the friend about it as I was sitting there. I wondered if I was having stroke or heart attack symptoms.

I had started seeing a counselor by this time to try to help me with my grief. She gave me an exercise that I've now learned much more about. She had me focus on my feet and focus that they were resting on the floor; or focus that my butt was sitting in the chair; or focus on the way the chair felt against my back. She was trying to teach me mindfulness, getting grounded in the present. I practiced that exercise a lot, and it seemed to help.

Since then, I've done much more work around mindfulness and have learned that it's a great pattern interrupter. My symptoms were probably a fight-or-flight response my body was having because it was so overwhelmed with all the thoughts going on in my head. The brain can't distinguish between something that's really happening right now and something we are just thinking about and fearing. For this reason my body was physically responding in fight-or-flight mode to the extreme fear and anxiety my brain was conjuring.

The most worrisome physical symptom was the strange heart stuff, especially at the Boys' UP Final High School Bowling Meet for Trevor's team. This took place in February within a month of Trevor's death. As I already explained, Trevor loved bowling and was part of the Ishpeming/Negaunee High School bowling team. This team was fabulous and often made it to the Michigan State Finals each year. We really enjoyed being part of that when both of our sons were on the team.

After Trevor's death the team invited us to be part of the UP Bowling Finals event, the purpose of which was to determine which teams and individuals would be moving on to the state-level competition. We wanted to be involved, so we could see Trevor's teammates and friends again, but we went reluctantly because we knew it would be extremely difficult to watch it without Trevor there.

We had such a huge outpouring of financial support from the community and family and friends after Trevor died that we decided to use some of the money to support things Trevor enjoyed. One of those things was the bowling team. I wrote a check to the team to support their trip to states. After the event, I walked over to the coach and his wife to hand over the check. I was feeling really happy about doing this—so what happened next was totally shocking.

As I was talking and handing the check over, I felt a painful surge in my chest, kind of like my heart was trying to push something out of it. Next my knees totally gave out under me, and I fell to the ground. Rob immediately grabbed me, and the coach's wife gave me a hug. Everyone was concerned about whether I was OK—me included! "Am I having a heart attack? What's going on?" I worried.

I didn't go to the emergency room or anything; instead I chose to relax and calm down during our 1.5-hour drive home. It was a very strange occurrence and one that hasn't happened since.

I explained this occurrence to Sherry, one of my closest friends who is a registered nurse with many years' experience in the healthcare field. Sherry explained to me something called "broken heart syndrome." I had never heard of it before. She said it was more common in a person grieving the loss of a spouse. She explained it had physical symptoms and affected the heart. I decided then that I would get a checkup at the doctor and get some blood tests done just to get some hard numbers in expectation that the results would decrease my worry.

My three surviving children had already been through so much that the last thing they needed was to have a sick mom!

I never had any problem with my heart after that which was as severe, but I started to worry about the other physical symptoms of all the grief and stress my body was enduring.

And it was strange—this contradictory mix of great worry I felt about my health and indifference to it, hoping I'd get cancer and die, so I could go be with Trevor. But that's the thing about grief—it doesn't make sense. It can't be pinned down and mapped out. It's all over the place.

7.
ALLIGATORS AND SNAKES

ANXIETY WAS SOMETHING I had never faced so severely before. It started small in those initial days. I started worrying whether any of my other kids might kill themselves. If Trevor—the straight-A student and kind, loving, thoughtful, and giving person—could do it, then it seemed possible that anyone else could too. And at any moment. These were thoughts that would come and go.

Things really came to a head when we took the kids on a trip to Florida within two months of losing Trevor. Rob's brother and sister-in-law were kind enough to let us use one of their timeshare weeks in Florida that year. We were grateful to be leaving the snow and house and grief behind for a week, but I was a little concerned that the trip would be a waste of money. How do you enjoy a vacation after enduring the suicide of your son?

When the time came, we drove to Trevor's grave and said good-bye to him. It was the first family vacation we were going on without him, and we felt the big empty space. Trevor loved family vacations and especially loved when we went to theme and roller coaster parks. He was the only one of us who dared to ride things like the Top Speed Dragster at Cedar Point, which he went on by himself and said was the best ride he'd ever experienced.

We wanted to honor what he would've liked to do, so we chose to go to Universal Studio's Islands of Adventure while we were in Florida. Its Harry Potter World was relatively new, and Trevor would've absolutely loved it.

It turned out to be the worst family vacation I'd ever been on. I was extremely jumpy and on edge the whole trip. Rob's driving seemed erratic to me, and I yelled a little too much about that. The radio seemed too loud, the songs seemed inappropriate for how we were feeling, and nothing seemed right. The condo we were staying in was gorgeous. Out the back patio door I could see a big, beautiful open area with lush greenery and a small waterway. However, when I looked out there, I pictured alligators and snakes coming up from the river and getting into our condo. It was absolutely terrifying.

When Kendra, who was 13 at the time, wanted to go out for a walk without me, I refused to let her go. All the bad things that could happen to her instantly came to mind: she'd get hit by a car or someone could come along and kidnap her or rape or kill her. Honestly, these thoughts were crushing any "fun" I could try to have on this vacation.

Then there was the theme park itself. I'm like a big kid at a theme park. The rides never get old, and I love the thrill of a good roller coaster. However, this time was very different. The Harry Potter ride would've been one Trevor would've totally loved. But, I went on it, I could barely open my eyes to enjoy it fully. Everything was over-the-top scary and seemed way too realistic for my tender state of grief at the time.

After the Harry Potter ride, I made a decision: I definitely could not participate in any roller coasters for the rest of the trip. Instead, I tried to squeeze enjoyment out of going on the smaller rides with our 8-year old, Annika. I envied that she could just seem to forget what had happened and have total wide-eyed wonderment about the theme park and all the wonderful experiences of the One Fish, Two Fish, Red Fish, Blue Fish ride, the Dr. Seuss trolley, and the Hippogriff roller coaster.

When Rob and Dylan were gone golfing, I was a nervous wreck. My mind was filled with horrible scenarios—a golf ball flying out of nowhere and nailing one of them in the face; or them getting in a car accident on the way back to the resort.

I slept extremely poorly and had a hard time adjusting to a family trip where Trevor wasn't with us.

I felt a lot of denial and confusion in those first months. For instance, I'd still think Trevor was going to come bounding down the stairs while I was sitting at the dining room table. He had this definite sound to his walk/run, which made him always seem to be in a hurry. Like he couldn't wait to get onto the next thing or back to the book he was reading or the music he was learning.

I also had thoughts that made me wonder if he'd ever existed. I'd have this real deep feeling that led me to believe he was a figment of my imagination. Many times I had to snap myself out of that thought pattern and look at the picture on the wall to realize he'd really been here.

My personal processing of his suicide and my family's new reality was something I resisted. I didn't want to be alone with my thoughts. I wanted to avoid them by watching TV and reading books late into the night. I binge watched TV shows at the beginning, trying not to think about what had happened. In fact, it seemed that the more ridiculous (fantasy and science fiction) a show's premise, the more I was drawn to it.

I read countless books about people losing their children, about near-death experiences, and about psychics who said they knew what was on the other side. I was drawn to sad and triumphant real-life stories about cults and read about four of those books in a row. I don't know precisely what I was craving, but reading allowed me to delve into someone else's life instead of facing what was going on in my own.

After denial, the guilt started, accompanied by sadness. Questions started surfacing in my head about what we had missed. What had we done wrong as parents? Had I not nursed Trevor long enough when he was a baby? (I quit nursing at six months but really believed I should've nursed him for a year.) How about those times he hit his head? We could think of several times that Trevor had hit his head really hard over his lifetime. We wondered if those head knocks had altered his brain chemistry in some way.

Then there was the guilt over not being a good enough Christian. Was God punishing us for something? I remember having lots of prayers and talks with God in my head, asking for answers to these questions.

When I couldn't find any answers through prayer, I started getting angry with God: where was he when my son Trevor needed help? Why didn't he put a voice in Trevor's head that told him to go tell someone about his pain? Why did something not happen to alert us that Trevor was in trouble?

Trevor had been the ultimate rule follower. Looking back on that, I feel like he followed rules even though he didn't believe in them, so he stuffed down his feelings so as not to let his parents down. He was so thoughtful that way, but it ended up costing him his life.

Anger came and went and came back again. I remember feeling angry at church. At first, I tried to be "normal" and go to church every weekend as before. I even tried to work in the church's kitchen for meals. What I couldn't handle was the normal chatter about "Did you hear that Ruth's son is moving to North Dakota because he got a job there?" and "Did you hear that Julie's daughter is getting married next summer?" or "Joan's daughter is having a baby, isn't that exciting?"

I felt like standing in the middle of the kitchen and screaming, "Does anyone remember that my son took a gun and shot himself!!!!?" The anger would build up little by little as I heard tidbits of conversation—and it felt totally overwhelming to me. So, I quit working in the church kitchen for meal times. In fact, I've quit going to church meals for the most part altogether unless it's a funeral or a wedding.

It was—and still is to a certain extent—the worst thing to see young people between the ages of 17 and 22 having a good time and moving on with their lives, knowing that our Trevor will never do those things. He'll never go to college, find a girlfriend, get married, have babies, have a career. It just gnaws away at me sometimes. Over the years that feeling is going away a little at a time, but my tears at weddings are usually about Trevor.

I was really angry for a long time about what I saw as a lack of support. It was like people tiptoed around us because they didn't want to remind us our son died. HELLO—we will NEVER forget that he died. And—we wanted to talk about it. We were just as confused as everyone else.

Sometimes I thought people were thinking we knew more than we were saying. NOPE! We were JUST as confused as they were, maybe more since we had been living in the very same house as him for almost 17.5 years, yet we really had no idea he had been depressed.

People would sometimes try to point out that we had other children to care for and live for. That was easy for them to say. All I could see was that I now had to deal with the effect of Trevor's suicide on my other children. Each of them had a different relationship with Trevor, and therefore, a different reaction. It seemed so unfair that they'd have to go through this suffering in life.

Whenever I saw other kids and parents celebrating their successes, I thought, "Well of course that kid did so great—they didn't have to deal with their brother dying of suicide." It was a mean thought that spun around my head for at least three years. Sometimes I still feel it creeping in and have to remember to change my language. It's only been a little over five years as of the writing of this book, but I'm cautiously optimistic that our other three children are doing OK.

In public I tried to put on a happy face most times. When people ask, "How are you doing?" usually they aren't hoping for a long story about what's going on in your head at the time. So, I became used to putting on a face and saying, "We're good" or "We're OK" or "We're doing as good as can be expected." If the person was a closer friend and I felt comfortable, I may share that things weren't that great. But I waffled between not wanting to drive people away and craving a shoulder to lean on and an ear to listen to me. And I'd come to rely on others for support because Rob and I weren't in a good place for one another at that time.

And that brings us to another fragile part of my life: the state of my marriage after the loss of our child.

8.

SAME BOOK, DIFFERENT PAGES

I HEARD SOMEONE say one time that what anyone thinks and feels isn't necessarily reality since each of us is seeing things from our own flawed perspective. This was especially true of Rob and me during this time.

What seemed especially difficult was that I couldn't get myself to understand Rob's deep anger. And he would ask me why I wasn't as angry or why I wasn't angry about the same things he was. With the passing of time, I realize that neither of us was right or wrong. We both had our own perspective of Trevor's death. Even though we lost the same son, our grief perspective was very different.

It's very difficult to see a person you love so much dealing with the loss of their son. I couldn't make it better for Rob, and he certainly couldn't make it better for me. Though I heard from some moms who've lost children to other causes that "my husband is my rock," I just couldn't see or feel that perspective during those first years.

During the first couple of weeks after Trevor died, Rob had an aura of spirituality and peace about him. I remember feeling very angry as he was trying to be the caretaker for everyone. I could hear him tell people on the phone, "We are doing OK, as well as can be expected" and "It's all going to be OK." I wanted everyone to know that I WAS NOT doing OK. I was extremely sad and spending lots of time in bed.

Now I believe the father in Rob was really doing his best to care for his family at that initial stage. Without him and that initial boost he had, the kids probably would've received nothing from us. And we needed Rob's boost to get all the details of the funeral and burial taken care of because as I already described, I was literally useless, unable to make decisions at that time.

I remember telling a couple of friends early on that I was worried for Rob. He seemed to be on a high, and I felt the imminent threat of his emotional crash.

When that emotional crash happened, I started to broaden my focus from my own sadness to worrying for Rob's sanity. I wonder if you ever really know a person until you see how they are during the deepest darkest period of loss. I was frightened by Rob's grief, and I was frightened by my actions.

I had nothing to offer to help Rob feel better (I couldn't do this for myself either). Rob would leave the house in anger really late at night sometimes just to go "drive around." There was nothing I could do to stop this, and I was terrified that he would do something stupid. I feared he was suicidal.

All I could do was pray really hard that God would watch over him and he'd return safely. I don't know what he did during those times, but I do understand the feeling of wanting to run from the pain.

Our marriage was a painful place to be at that time. We were shaping ourselves into two totally new people, people who had to learn to survive with a deep hole in our hearts. And this created a new marriage.

Rob was (and is) a great provider and stable pillar of strength for me in our marriage. He's my best friend, someone whom I can tell anything to and know he will always be on my side and supportive.

But, during that dark phase, I lost that Rob.

The overwhelming fear of never having that Rob back was crushing. That fear took me away from focusing on my own grief for a period of about a year. I was trying to figure out how to get our marriage and our kids through Rob's anger and pain. Rob is an engineer, and used to solving problems. The puzzle of Trevor's death was unsolvable, and that seemed to be the sticking point for him.

I remembered wondering one time if it would really be against God's law if we got divorced because we weren't the same people that had promised our love to each other in August 1991. Separation was a topic that we first discussed after Trevor died. We had already been married for almost 20 years and had been through ups and downs, but no down was worse than this. The insecurity I felt was unlike anything else.

On my part, I made a conscious decision that I was going to keep my vow. I was going to love and honor him in sickness and in health—no matter what. No matter how tough it got, I needed to stick with it. I kept telling myself that it could only get better.

Each of us had separate counselors at that time. We resisted doing counseling together. I remember inviting Rob to come with me to one session with my counselor. He told me later that he felt like he was being "ganged up on" by me and my counselor, so didn't want to go back.

I can see his point now. I was trying everything to change his behavior. I just wanted him back to the way he was before. And, I'm sure he would've liked me to be different too. We were trying everything there was to figure out how to exist inside the new marriage.

I beat myself up for a while because I couldn't figure out how to fix the marriage. In my alone moments, I'd try to figure out how I wanted to act around Rob so that his anger would be abated. I'd even come up with a strategy, some "adult-like" talking points. Then, as soon as I had the chance to interact with him, all hell would break loose again, I'd be triggered by something he said, and my good intentions would go right out the window. I'm not afraid to raise my voice, yell and scream, and stomp my feet like an angry teenager.

I'm embarrassed to say that this behavior happened more often than not during our fights back then. The only thing I can think now is I was trying to manipulate him to be the Rob that would do his best to give me what I wanted.

Rob and I never seemed to be in the same stage of grieving. He was angry, I was sad. I was angry, he was in problem-solving mode and trying to convince me we were going to be all right.

You always read about the "stages of grief." Well, I can tell you that there's no specific path to go down to get through the stages. In fact, you may think you're done with one stage, but it comes right back and you feel like you are starting all over again. Weird and strange. And, as I already stated, Rob and I never seemed to be in the same stage at the same time.

9.
TOO BLESSED?

BEFORE TREVOR DIED—I felt we were incredibly blessed. I remember many times thinking, "That's untrue," when I'd hear someone say, "Life isn't supposed to be easy. We are supposed to suffer through great trials." I never believed that.

I started reading loads of self-help books during my twenties and have kept that up for years. I always believed we are all meant to be here for a reason and do great things. Whatever great gifts we each have, we are supposed to share those with the world. There was no way for me to accept that life is supposed to be difficult when I was consistently reading success stories about others. Lots of those people had overcome terrible life things to be successful.

After Trevor died—I went through a period of time saying, "I guess we were too blessed." I had always felt that we had the perfect-size family: two boys and two girls; two redheads and two blondes. Who could ask for anything more? I felt blessed that we were living the middle-class American dream in a small town in Upper Michigan. There were always the normal money problems and marital fights, but to me that was a normal part of the sweet life.

When Trevor died, my rosy picture of what life was supposed to be was shattered. I remember asking many times, "OK, God, now what?"

In fact, we had gone regularly to church, brought our children to Sunday school, and tried our darnedest to follow the "rules" we thought would please God. So, after Trevor died—I had a crisis of faith. I felt like possibly everything I had done up to that point was totally wrong: was I in the right faith? Did I go to the right church? Trevor was brought up in our church, so maybe we had everything wrong. We'd taught Trevor about God and about "doing the right thing" and about obeying his elders. Why wasn't God there to help when Trevor needed him?

Rob and I blamed ourselves: why didn't we see that something was wrong? Why would my motherly instinct not know there was something wrong? In one of his poems that we saw later, Trevor wrote that he was depressed and not sleeping—why didn't we know he wasn't sleeping well?

I remember saying it over and over again after he died, "When would you think to check in on your 17-year old son every night to see if he's in bed sleeping?" When he shut his door to his room, I assumed he was sleeping.

I was really concerned for a while, and I put tremendous blame on myself. You see, Trevor had been in our bedroom in the early morning hours that Sunday of his death. I know this because I was faintly aware of someone opening the drawers to the built-in dresser that was across from our bed. It didn't startle me because we kept a bottom drawer with kids' movies and sometimes one of our daughters would wake up earlier on the weekends and find a movie to watch in the family room.

My half-asleep brain knew someone was there but didn't bother getting up to check it out. I often think about what would've happened if I had woken up at that time. Would I have known what Trevor's intention was? Would he have told me what he was doing?

There's a list of circumstances I remind myself of to try and make myself accept this horrible tragedy—and not blame myself:

1. When Trevor got the gun, I was half-awake but felt no need to fully wake up to see what was happening.

2. When Trevor shot himself around 7 am (we know this because his friends received a good-bye text from Trevor around 7 am), all of us were sleeping in the house and didn't hear a thing.

3. Our dog Teddy's kennel was right outside Trevor's door. He never made a sound.

These are the circumstances around that Sunday morning. One could come to the conclusion that it was meant to happen this way—that it wasn't my and Rob's faults.

Someone later made the comment that God had closed our ears to the horrible sound. I agree. As the angels came to take our Trevor away, we were all blissfully unaware and deeply asleep.

Even still, acceptance didn't and doesn't come easily. My mind wanted to fight it at every turn. I had arguments inside my head: I'd say, "Well, it was meant to be because . . . ," and then the other voice would interrupt, "That's crazy! Why would God choose our son to die by suicide? He had so much potential, that's so unfair" or "Why couldn't he have died in a car accident if it was his time to go?" or "Even cancer would've been so much more acceptable to everyone, and then we would've received so much better support."

Our oldest son Dylan told Rob, "God doesn't make mistakes." In his way, Dylan was trying to help us accept that Trevor was on his own path, and it wasn't our fault or anyone else's. God chose that Trevor had to die like this for some reason.

During some slivers of time in the early years, I'd feel this huge rush of peace and acceptance. I'd be so grateful that one of my children was now safely in heaven and didn't have to face the terrible sorrow and fears and tragic things that happen in this life.

10.
DREAMS AND GHOSTS

DREAMS WERE SORT of a weird and comforting thing. Rob says he still hasn't had any dreams about Trevor. But, I did. I kept a separate journal where I'd record my dreams.

I remember after Trevor died in those first days I had a dream that Rob and I were driving down the road. All of a sudden, I noticed Trevor sitting in the backseat quietly behind me. In my dream he was about 9 or 10 years old. He didn't say anything when I looked at him, so I looked at Rob and asked, "What's he doing here? He's dead!" Rob replied with something like "Maybe he's stuck between worlds right now."

I'd wake up from these dreams and wonder if Trevor was trying to get a message to me. Was he trying to make me feel better before he finally went to heaven permanently? It was so confusing.

My very favorite dream of Trevor was also quite strange. I was going into our master bathroom, which is an unusually large room. For some reason, my nieces and nephews and other friends of theirs were having a party in the master bath (remember, it's a dream). I went up to look for my niece. When I walked into the bathroom, it was like none of the other kids existed.

Standing quietly in the corner of the bathroom was Trevor. He was looking at me intently. Again, he couldn't have been more than 10 or 11.

I said, "Trevor, come here."

He walked over to me and I put my arms around him and pulled him into my chest. His head was resting on my chest below my chin far enough that I could close my eyes and rest my head on top of his.

I told him, "Trevor, I love you and miss you."

The feeling of hugging him and the love I felt for him was so intense that I still felt it when I woke up and realized it was just a dream.

The only dream where Trevor said anything to me was one time when I dreamt he was bounding down the stairs to the fridge like he always did. I turned around to see him (once again, I always knew in my dreams that he was dead) and asked, "Trevor, are you OK?" (like "Why are you here?"). He responded in his usual flippant voice, "Yep!" And that was that. That dream made me feel he was OK.

I believe deeply that there are ghosts and signs from beyond that we just can't see. This started with my baby brother's death from cancer back in 1997. After Darin died, there was this interesting spot that would show up in lots of family pictures. A fuzzy gray spot. We could only surmise that it was Darin.

My mom and dad said they get signs from Darin off and on (and now they include Trevor in those visits): the radio or TV would turn itself on, and they'd say that my brother was visiting.

We had an electrical issue that lends itself to this kind of story. For some reason, before Trevor died, something had happened to the wiring that went into Trevor's room and our girls' room (which was next to Trevor's). Kendra noticed it and said that she couldn't turn on the overhead light. I don't recall if Trevor ever reported it. However, he always played a song titled "Bink's Sake" on his keyboard every night before going to bed. He wasn't able to play it for a couple of nights. I guess we hadn't realized that the power in his room was totally out the day he died and maybe for a day or two before that.

When all the friends and family were at our house on that initial Sunday, Rob took a group of guys (who are all very knowledgeable about wiring) into the basement to try and figure out how to get the power to work again. They did everything you normally would do—flip the breakers and such—to no avail. Every day Rob would monkey with the power trying to get the lights to go on, but nothing would happen.

Several days or even a week after the funeral, which was one to two weeks since Trevor had died, Rob came running upstairs excitedly saying that the power was back on in Trevor's room. There was no rhyme or reason as to why it was back—it was just back! He hadn't done anything different than before. We realized, kind of sadly, that Trevor was then truly gone. Maybe he had stuck around in that room for a while to make sure we were OK.

Dylan had been in the bedroom after Trevor died and felt Trevor's presence there so strongly telling Dylan it would be OK. When Dylan relayed this to us, we felt very comforted by that.

Another time, Rob's sister had written us a note to say that she didn't know why but she had gotten this message that would not leave her alone. She tried over and over to ignore the message over several days, not wanting us to think she was crazy or anything. The message came to her while she had been visiting her Granny's grave (Granny had a bit of a sixth sense about her). The message was simply "I'm OK, Dad. It's OK."

Now that might not make sense to anyone until you find out that Rob had had a terribly troubling day a few days before this note arrived in the mail. He had been driving around crying and trying to figure out why Trevor's suicide had happened. He asked Trevor to please send him a sign that he was OK.

The hardest thing as parents of a child who died is feeling that we weren't done raising him—and that now he's out there somewhere all alone without our guidance. It just felt wrong. So, this note from Rob's sister gave us so much peace and a feeling that Trevor really was with us—we just couldn't see him.

11.
Helping Hands

WHEN I FINISHED college, I got on this bandwagon of learning from other people about different things. I went through an extreme couponing phase when I was a stay-at-home mom with Dylan in those first years of marriage. Next, when I saw the infomercial for Carleton Sheets' real estate course, I started down the path of learning everything I could to become a real estate magnate. After that, I got hooked on reading Tony Robbins and Zig Ziglar books. Suffice it to say that I became a self-help junkie in my early twenties (something I shared earlier in the book). So, getting help is not beyond me.

However, after Trevor's death, it took a couple of months for me to acknowledge that I would need help then too. It became crystal clear to me while we were in Florida on that vacation I described already. The anxiety I felt on the trip was enough to make me finally admit that I needed help. I needed help sleeping, and I needed help with my anxiety.

Medical Doctor

First, I got a checkup from the doctor, and he prescribed anti-anxiety medication for my anxiety and depression. The long-term effects of getting little and broken sleep really had me feeling quite loopy, so the doctor also gave me Ambien to help me sleep.

I often blame that medication for the first 25 pounds of weight I gained after Trevor died—never mind the self-medication of bags of chocolate candy. After all, as I already shared, my thinking at the time was "What's the point of being healthy when my son just died?" It seemed like such a petty thing to worry about at the time, and sugar became a crutch for me.

Counselor

After a time, I felt that the medication wasn't enough, and I really needed to talk about everything that was going on. Rob and I were just at different places in our grief. I needed to find out how I could help him since I barely could help myself. I found a counselor who had lost her 16-year-old son in a car accident many years earlier. I felt that at least she'd understand the pain of losing a teenage son. I spent many times crying and talking in her office. It was a relief to just talk to a neutral party who had no background on our family.

Talking to my friends was OK, but they had their own thoughts about what I should or shouldn't do sometimes, and I really just needed someone who wasn't attached in any way to listen to all the weird things I was thinking and feeling. She gave me a safe place to come and dump everything, and that was the real beginning of my understanding about grief.

Compassionate Friends

Another place I went was the local Compassionate Friends chapter. Compassionate Friends is a national organization that was put together for parents who've lost a child. Our chapter met monthly but was very small. The first time I showed up, there was the leader and one other person. As I had heard that you should give a group three tries before you decide it's not for you, I kept going to the meetings and ended up going every single month for at least a year.

The good thing about Compassionate Friends is we all found a common bond: we had lost our children too young. It was against the laws of nature to have our children go before us. We heard from others who had the same feelings we did about dumb things people said to us. We also all had some of the same bizarre thoughts in our heads, so it was helpful to know that I wasn't going crazy—I was simply grieving.

National Compassionate Friends Conference

I decided to go the National Compassionate Friends conference when it was held in Chicago a couple of summers after Trevor died. That was where I really felt uplifted and helped since each type of death had its own group meetings and learning sessions. That's where I learned that lots of people who die by suicide are "normal." And, lots of them do it without letting on that they are deeply troubled.

I learned there that high achievers and perfectionists sometimes die by suicide. Also, I learned that the suicide rates in students in medical schools are higher than in other programs. Dana Cook Grossman's article "Reducing the Stigma: Faculty Speak Out about Suicide Rates among Students, Physicians" from September 2016 on the Association of American Medical Colleges news page states:

> Higher suicide rates among physicians than in the general population are widely documented. How much higher is not clear because solid data are lacking, experts agree. But Srijan Sen, MD, PhD, an assistant professor of psychiatry at the University of Michigan Medical School and the principal investigator of the Intern Health Study, a longitudinal study of

depression among interns nationwide, estimates "suicide rates among physicians are something like 40 to 70 percent higher in males and 130 to 300 percent higher in women. (https://news.aamc.org/medical-education/article/reducing-stigma-suicide-rates/)

From all this information I started to feel comforted that Trevor wasn't "nuts." He had some depression that he couldn't deal with—but that didn't make him a bad person. For some reason, I'd had this fear in the back of my head that I had a child who was severely mentally ill and I'd totally missed every sign—and it was all my fault. I started to lose the grip on that thought when I went to the conference and found out about all the "normal" kids and adults, even doctors and medical students, who had also died by suicide.

At the conference we had a lovely dinner in a ballroom with about a thousand people. We also had a candle lighting ceremony to honor our dead children. There was bagpipe music and soft candlelight. It was the most love I felt in a room of people since Trevor had died. I felt a real spiritual connection there that I hadn't before.

I think it was the first time I felt some hope that I could do this: I can grieve for Trevor and feel connected to him. And I can feel connected to God and know that he is still the loving God I've always thought he was.

I also got the idea that we had to do a balloon release at Trevor's grave that summer. It would be his twentieth birthday, and I wanted to do something that felt good.

Balloons Up and Away

On August 3, 2014, we invited all of Trevor's friends, the bowling team, some of our friends, some work friends, and our families to Trevor's gravesite.

It turned out to be a beautiful day, sunny with a mild breeze. About 75 people showed up. We had a couple of super talented kids sing some songs at the graveside, and then we all released our balloons with their written messages for Trevor on them. It was beautiful.

Afterwards we had people to our home for Trevor's favorite foods: grilled hot dogs, hamburgers, baked beans, and homemade hot fudge sauce on vanilla ice cream. That day, the day of Trevor's 20th birthday, will always stick in my memory as an anti-funeral. It's what I would've liked to do on the day of Trevor's funeral, but I guess we wouldn't have been ready to do that then.

Other Support

We tried to get help in other ways. There is a Survivors of Suicide group that we attended once. The one time we attended, there was only the leader and one other person. That other person had not lost a child, and we really didn't feel much of a connection. But to be fair, I didn't give this group the three tries as I had the Compassionate Friends group.

We did go to the American Foundation for Suicide Prevention's Out of the Darkness Community Walk several years in a row. They have a balloon release there which feels nice.

One year we got a team of people together to come to the walk with us, and I felt so much support. What I learned from those walks is that the community needs to be better educated on the fact that suicide is about a brain illness. Brain illnesses are just as "normal" as physical ailments. Our children and others with mental ailments are not getting the help they need. For one thing, it's stigmatizing to ask for help for something that's not a physical illness. There is a real lack of teaching on mental illness in our communities.

A great source of help, and one we hadn't anticipated, consisted of the opening, sorting, and responding to all the cards we received. I don't remember how many, but there were definitely somewhere over 400 cards. It was tremendous, and I was grateful that people remembered that we had lost someone even though it was by a "socially unacceptable method" like suicide.

The outpouring of love from the students at the high school was also amazing. Trevor's friends and classmates poured out their love to us. Riley, a real sweet classmate of his, was allowed to collect notes from students at Trevor's locker. She put together an album for us, which contained special poems, letters, and pictures. I treasure these things. Those friends did everything they could in their young lives to tell us how much they cared.

Overall, I truly believe I'm way farther on my healing path now than I could've been if I hadn't sought out help. Counselors, therapists, and grief support groups exist for the very purpose of helping those who are facing these unfathomable losses. It seems that some of them are like a really well-kept secret. I hope that if you are reading this, you'll use some of these tools or pass them along to those who need them.

Eventually there came a period of time where I felt all "helped" out. I was then ready to start to take some actions on my own to find joy in my life. I can't say that the things I've done for myself have been easy, but they are very worth it. In the next chapter I'll talk about what I started doing in order to shift my focus more on joy than on sorrow.

12.
THE BIG "AHA"

A CRUCIAL WAY I tried to help myself with my grief was by decluttering. Decluttering is a huge passion of mine. To me, it's a foundational method for making important strides in life to become better, live better, and get to the next level. Whether we are talking about grief or starting a business or writing a book—any goal we want to reach has to start with decluttering.

I only realized this after Trevor died.

While I love organizing things, what I've learned is organizing isn't the same as decluttering. Decluttering entails not simply throwing things out but releasing them too. It means releasing physical things, things on your schedule, mental things, and emotional things. Releasing a bunch of "stuff" through decluttering has helped me to find creativity, inspiration, and joy, and has ultimately given me freedom from the debilitating effects of grief. That's huge, so let me explain.

Physical decluttering is the easiest thing and probably the thing that comes to mind when I say the word "declutter," so we'll start with physical decluttering, meaning decluttering your surroundings.

Overall, I went through some very dark periods of time since Trevor died, and sometimes the physical clutter really piled up on me. It's almost as if what was going on inside me led to clutter in my physical surroundings. And, in turn, that clutter seemed to crush my spirit, which led to more clutter, and on and on—a negative spiral.

So how to stop the spiral? How to remove myself from it?

I've read many "organizing" books over the years and have tried many different methods to organize my physical space. You know, buying all the containers to make the space look pretty, etc. However, after reading *The Life-Changing Magic of Tidying Up: The Japanese Art of Decluttering and Organizing* by Marie Kondo, I had a shift in my thinking around organizing. From this book, an aha moment came to me: I realized that my physical space can feel icky even if it's organized in boxes. If there's a bunch of stuff sitting around that's not working for where you are in life at the moment, then everything can feel overwhelming—even if all that stuff is "organized."

Here are my rules for how to determine what I keep versus get rid of:

1. It doesn't fit anymore (too big or small).

2. It tends to stay buried at the bottom of things and I never feel like wearing or using it.

3. I got it as a gift a long time ago and am keeping it out of guilt.

4. It doesn't FEEL GOOD when I touch it.

This last one may sound strange, but if you really get quiet as you are doing your decluttering and listen to your thoughts about things you touch while decluttering, you will receive inner guidance on whether an item fits into your life at this point or not.

Because I want to feel really good about every item that's in my home and my closet, every item must meet all four of the criteria.

I have always had this issue with closets. Some way they never feel clean or right to me. I refuse to spend several thousand dollars on one of those fancy closet systems since that's probably not the real issue.

From Marie Kondo's book and the four rules I derived from it, I finally learned how to keep my closet clean on a level beyond the physical. This happened a couple of years ago at a time when I was grasping at anything to try to make my life feel better. Since reading her book, my closet has been organized, decluttered, clean, and feels amazing when I walk into it every morning, all of which gives me a distinct sense of ease and gets my day started on the right foot.

All the clothes that are in my closet fit me for the body size I am right now. That's half the battle. I've come to the point of immediately putting a clothing item into the Goodwill bag as soon as I think it doesn't fit or I simply don't like it for any reason whatsoever. That way, I keep a decluttered space, and I don't have clothes sitting around "just because."

This also honors me for who I am and where I am in my journey right now. Even though I'm not at what I would consider a "healthy weight," I am honoring my body right now. I am loving myself by allowing myself to keep clothing that fits me well. If I keep clothing that's a size or two too small, then I'm giving myself the sign that I don't accept me for where I am today. Also, if I keep clothing on hand that I've shrunk out of, then I'm telling myself I don't trust that I am going to honor my commitment to continue getting healthier. Living with the body I have right now is one of the best ways I can love myself. And by loving myself, I am best positioned to love my husband, children, and everyone in this world—which means I'm able to live the most authentic and amazing life possible.

Physical-space decluttering also helped me tackle my workspace. I work from home now, so it's important that I have a clear mind when I'm writing a book, creating blog posts, or filming videos. Being overwhelmed with clutter everywhere makes me instead want to focus on cleaning house instead of building my business. I've learned that this is called "buffering": using an excuse like cleaning or organizing instead of dealing with the discomfort I feel when putting myself out on the internet through videos or blog posts. (And yes, it is an ongoing process. I might write another book about it when I actually figure it out more completely! ☺)

When I declutter, I use a garbage bag, a timer, a box for giving things to Goodwill, and a basket to bring things back where they belong. I set a timer for as little as 15 minutes. Then I promise myself to do 15 minutes a day if that's what it takes to get the space decluttered. If I have more time I set aside two to four hours to get it all done at once.

It's weird what a pile of stuff does to us mentally and emotionally. However, decluttering isn't only applied to our physical surroundings. When I learned to apply it to myself in terms of decluttering my schedule, my mental habits, and my emotional patterns, I found even greater ease, peace, and stability, something we'll explore in the next chapter.

13.
METAPHYSICAL DECLUTTERING

Schedule Decluttering

HOW OFTEN HAVE you thought about everything you are obligated to in your life and how it fits in with your true purpose or your dreams and goals? I tend to clutter my schedule with stuff that keeps me running around constantly. Only in the last six months have I gotten super clear about what I will and won't say yes to.

A powerful way to make decisions about new things that come into your life is to first ask yourself if the new thing fits with one of your goals. For instance, I've now decided that I don't need to be involved in every church function or participate in every church meal to believe in God. That was a huge weight off my shoulders. Instead, I choose to play the organ and serve at certain weddings and funerals. This makes me feel like I'm really serving in a way that is giving the best of myself. When I feel like I'm doing a bunch of things because "I have to," then I get resentful. And, I don't think charitable giving is supposed to make me feel resentful.

I had a load of guilt (even brought on by other people) when I started saying no to church duties. But, instead of letting fear or guilt make decisions for me and have me regress back to being the people pleaser again, I stood strong and politely said no.

I'm sad that it's taken until my mid-forties to really think about stuff like this. I realize there are so many things I could be volunteering for and helping with, but I need to be picky because my time is precious. I want to make sure I have time for myself, my husband, my family, my friends, and my business. Cluttering my schedule with unwanted obligations leads me to feel overwhelmed, not good enough, guilty, resentful, exhausted, and depressed.

Now that my schedule is decluttered, I have time to write books, go on weekend dates with my hubby, take trips with my daughters, meet friends for lunch regularly, serve on a nonprofit board, read books I love, and grow a business. I still have to struggle daily with making decisions about what to say yes and no to, but I'm so much clearer around what my goals are; therefore, I can say yes to the right things.

Mental Decluttering

The third area where I have done decluttering work since Trevor died is in regard to mental stuff—letting go of things like limiting beliefs, wrong perceptions, self-hate, feelings of failure, loads of guilt, and unreasonable expectations. This mental decluttering work has been a long process.

Initially, I tried to let this stuff go by talking about it at lunch to friends and on the phone to my sister. Those were conversations filled with emotion and tears. I appreciated the listening ears but didn't feel like any of those people truly understood where I was coming from. Really, how could they? I felt I needed a professional who wasn't so close to me that could tell me if I was crazy. Some of the things I thought were just outright ridiculous.

I've let a lot of that stuff go, so it's hard to recreate all those crazy thoughts now, but I'll try to recall some examples. For instance, I remember wondering, "If there really is a God, why does he make life so miserable?" And I had recurring thoughts of made-up "bad things" happening in my life or to the people I love. For example, if Rob was going out of town for work, I was overly afraid he'd get in a car accident. If Dylan was going out with friends, I became preoccupied by the fear that they'd be hit by a drunk driver. If Kendra had some sort of physical pain, I immediately worried it was cancer. Also I had recurring thoughts about someone getting into our house and hurting us.

Some of my darkest thoughts I could not see myself sharing with family or friends, so I talked with a counselor regularly for about two years. While she helped in many ways, I often felt unsettled with it all.

A great technique called EFT entered my life and helped me let go of lots of inner clutter. EFT stands for emotional freedom technique. Some may call it "woo woo," but I call it fabulous! I learned about it many years ago when I first started poking around for weight loss and health stuff online. However, I never really got into it fully at that time.

I was reintroduced to the emotional freedom technique (EFT or tapping, as I'll explain) by John Gabriel, the weight-loss expert behind the Gabriel Method. I came to John Gabriel and the Gabriel Method after trying many things over many years to lose weight. So, before I talk to you about EFT, I'll share a brief history of me and my body, one that I expect many women will relate to.

I have faced issues with my body since Dylan, my first child, was born when I was 21 years old. Before that I never had a weight issue. I've thought about this often and have finally come to the realization that for some reason I started hating my body when it was sort of out of shape after having a baby. Instead of embracing it for the wonderful thing it just did, i.e., growing and nurturing and birthing a baby, I was looking at loose belly skin and misshapen breasts and thinking, "Yuck . . . you are ugly."

Even before my pregnancy with Dylan, I had a problematic relationship with sugar. I started a love affair with chocolate as a child, but the issues with it seemed to become more pronounced during sad or lonely times in my life. Candy and desserts were my companions, especially after Trevor died. When Trevor died, I was an active participant in Weight Watchers and had just lost 19 pounds over a period of time. I was feeling pretty fantastic with having a handle on food and had the goal to lose about 50 more pounds. Then Trevor died and all that was pushed by the wayside. In fact, I totally forgot I was ever even on a program: what was the difference what weight I was when my son had just decided to leave this world so I could never see him again? The thought about food and eating healthy just seemed totally ridiculous in that new reality.

So, little by little the weight started creeping back on. And, I started keeping bags of chocolate candy bars, Hershey's Kisses, and M&M's within reach. I easily fell back into a habit of bingeing on sugar. I'd eat a bag of candy, then feel unwell, and vow to not eat another bag for the next whole week! But, before I knew it, I was looking around for sugar again and breaking my promise to myself.

The worst of the bingeing came during stressful times in my job. Especially during the three months' audit period each year. I had three months of bingeing on chocolate to a) keep my energy up for long 12- to 14-hour days and b) to "reward" myself because I was doing this hard job and bringing money home to my family even when I wasn't feeling fulfilled by the work anymore.

Several times I tried to get a handle on it. I tried to go back to Weight Watchers for a while. But, it wasn't the program that I couldn't handle. The problem I found was that I had a hard time participating in some things that had existed in my "normal" world, the one that Trevor had been in. Now that he was no longer here, things like Weight Watchers became very painful. They were a stark reminder that when I'd been there before, Trevor had still been alive.

I tried a lot of other things. I tried to contain my sugar to one day per week. I tried exercising every morning before work hoping that would stave off sugar cravings. I read somewhere that I might be low on magnesium if I was craving chocolate all the time, so I started taking magnesium supplements. My naturopathic doctor gave me a natural remedy supplement that was supposed to help with cravings. I went on several different ten-day detoxes that were supposed to clean the cravings out of my system. I did the "Whole 30" diet one year and ended up resentful of all the time I had to spend in the kitchen making fancy meals and sauces to make the diet work.

When my doctor recommended John Gabriel's book and the Gabriel Method as a way for me to lose weight, I decided to give it a try. The method also included an online course component as well as one-on-one coaching with John Gabriel himself.

During a call-in coaching session, I was able to talk directly to John on the phone, and I broke down crying because I told him my son died of suicide and I knew that was the reason I couldn't lose weight. I will forever be grateful that he told me to stop doing anything in his weight-loss book and find a tapping coach instead. (Shortly, I'll explain tapping, how it works, and why it was right for me.)

Before I found the tapping coach, I learned from John Gabriel that our body is built to protect us. When we experience a huge tragedy, all those thoughts, feelings, and emotions that come afterwards make our brain stay in the fight-or-flight mode. In that mode, our body conserves every bit of fat it has for survival. Even if the event happened several years ago, our brain doesn't know any different.

Recently, I got into the habit of being grateful for my body, which I now understand was protecting me through this whole mess of five years. I started to love it for what it was, and that has put me on the right path to health.

Before I go into EFT and how it has helped me, both in terms of my body issues and my grief, I want to mention guilt. Guilt was another important emotion I needed to declutter—guilt for not knowing what was happening, guilt for not being available like I should be for my other children while I was in the dark pit of despair, guilt for thinking maybe if I was a better mom overall this never would've happened. That sort of thinking also suggested that I actually had control.

Losing a child to suicide never fit into my picture of how the world worked and how the things that I did influenced what my children did. It was just another thing to grieve over: the total realization that I am not in control threw me for a loop for the entire first year. My whole view of life got turned on its head, and I wasn't sure what I should think or feel or believe anymore.

As mentioned already, John Gabriel directed me to EFT and tapping as the go-to method for decluttering the turmoil and confusion that I was experiencing. Whether it was stress and anxiety in terms of my body, Trevor's death, or my marriage, or anything else, I worked with a tapping coach to learn how to process the discomfort.

After learning the EFT and tapping process, I would analyze what I was feeling and write it down on paper. I thought about what the feeling was, as well as the thought behind it. When I felt guilt, for example, I reminded myself that I was allowed to feel guilt, but I also needed to know that I have always done the best I can, with the information I've been given. I can't do better than that. Even if there were some things that could be legitimately argued that I should've done differently, the past cannot be changed.

I learned to tap (see the process in the next section) and say aloud the things I felt guilty about. And I let myself really feel the guilt deeply. I've learned you cannot let a feeling go without acknowledging it and letting it run through you. I then turned those negative feelings of guilt into positive thoughts and beliefs. Then I'd tap over and over again using positive affirmations like "I did the best I could with the information I had" and "I am a loving person who is doing the very best I can."

Ultimately I had to repeat a forgiveness mantra in order to forgive myself for all the pain I had been inflicting upon myself: "I forgive you, I'm sorry, thank you, I love you." This forgiveness mantra hangs on the wall inside my bedroom closet where I can read it every morning and every night.

Through all the mental decluttering work I did, I have come to be a much stronger, more reasonable thinking adult. I now have a much better perspective on life. And I am at peace with the thought of death. Trevor is waiting for me on the other side, but I'm going to be patient and spend the time here on Earth in the best way I can.

Emotional Decluttering

The last thing to declutter was the emotional stuff. Of course that includes grief, anger, hatred, resentment, and fear. Tapping and EFT, which I touched on earlier, really helped me do this emotional decluttering.

Tapping works like this:

1. I'd think of something in my head that was really bothering me. For instance, something a certain person said to me after Trevor died that I couldn't let go of.

2. I'd notice what feeling that brought in my body. For example, in my body, I could feel things in my stomach, like a clenching feeling.

3. I'd rate the feeling from 1–10. How much did it really bother me? Ten was the top of the scale.

4. Then I'd start a tapping routine with my coach. She'd come up with the words based on what I told her was bothering me, and I'd just repeat after her. And at the same time I'd tap a particular point on my body.

5. The first three things I'd always say while tapping on the midpoint area on the outside of my left hand was something along the lines of: "Even though [Name] said this to me and it really makes me angry, I completely and totally love and accept myself."

6. In addition to the area on the outside of the hand, there are eight other tapping sites on the face, collarbone, under the arm, and on the top of the head. I'd tap along with my coach on the anger that I was feeling around a specific thing. We'd tap several rounds.

7. I tapped several such "negative" rounds, all the while saying, "This makes me angry" and "I can't believe they said that." Lots of times tears would come during these sessions—and that was a good thing. I was releasing pent up emotion that was locked inside my cells.

8. We'd check in with my stomach again to see what the level of feeling was. If it had gone down enough (like from a 10 to a 5 or lower), then we would switch to a "positive" round in which I'd say, "It's OK; people don't know what to say" or "They don't mean to hurt me; they want to help" or "I forgive them; they just have no idea what I'm feeling," etc.

9. By the end of the tapping round, my coach would ask if anything came up during that round, and ALWAYS something else came up. It was like following a squiggly maze. In fact, the thing that came up next may or may not be related as much to the thing I had just been tapping on. For example, I'd be tapping on some anger I was feeling about my job at the time, and suddenly something that happened during middle school would pop up. It was fascinating. My tapping coach said the best way to find out why we were feeling certain things was to always follow wherever our thoughts led. Maybe instances in my past were bringing up behaviors and things I was facing in myself in the present. So cool!

EFT deals with the body's energy system. Tapping uses acupuncture points to clear the energy that was "stuck" by negative emotions. When this energy is stuck, it can cause mental and physical pain in the body. So, clearing the stuck emotions allows the energy of the body to be rebalanced, thus leading to better physical and mental health.

You don't need to understand why tapping works in order for it to be effective for you. I hired a tapping coach because I'm generally one that is willing to have someone help me work on a problem right now and see immediate results. Also, I want help with very specific issues, and a coach helped me with those.

If you want to try it out on yourself for the first time, look up Brad Yates on YouTube. There are many others, but I find that he does tapping on a variety of topics, and he has a gentle nature that I find soothing.

Now I enjoy tapping on my own, anything that is top of mind gets tapped on. For example, I may tap on things like stage fright before presenting at a workshop, anger that comes up when Rob and I are having a heated discussion, or my fear around success when I do goal-setting work related to my business. I have also used tapping for reducing hunger when I know I'm not truly physically hungry.

It's amazing how I can change my perspective on an overpoweringly negative feeling or thought I've gotten in my head. I always tend to tell myself that when something bad happens, it must have something to do with me: "That happened because I'm a bad person, God doesn't love me, that person hates me, I'm just not good enough, etc." Now, with this tapping technique, I lose any negative, self-punishing feelings and beliefs. I release them to find peace, calm, and self-acceptance.

I have learned that consistently decluttering my mental space is really important to keep emotional balance, stay in touch with who I really am, and allow room for more happiness in my life. As I finally cleared out a lot of mental and emotional "stuff," I finally made room for self-love.

14.
LOVE MYSELF TIME

I REMEMBER SEEING a counselor, Mary, in order to try to find peace and joy in the job I was at. There were some difficulties at the job, and I was having a hard time wanting to stay. After several sessions with the counselor, I remember very clearly her saying that she was on my side in all this—but that I wasn't even on my own side.

I thought about that a lot: "If I don't even like myself enough to stick up for me, why would anyone else?" That was one of the biggest life lessons in my learning to love myself, and I am grateful to Mary for shedding a light on it.

There were so many things that have kept me from loving myself. My perfection about things became a big block at times. I have always had high expectations of relationships, vacations, events, and how things will go. "What did I do wrong that these things are going wrong for me on this trip?" One time my plane was delayed from flying from Marquette, Michigan, to Las Vegas for a conference I was attending. The flight was delayed by two days! And, I made up a big story around it, "I should never go on these trips anyway, I don't deserve to have a nice trip, etc."

These high expectations really brought me down when Trevor died. No way, no how does a child who is depressed and dies by suicide fit into my expectation of what our future would hold. I had rosy pictures of four kids who all got college degrees, good jobs, found a Christian spouse to marry, and had four kids of their own. I dreamed of taking grandchildren on vacations and going on Disney trips with the whole crew of us. These are the dreams that have been shattered. Once again, I felt like I must've done something wrong—everyone else gets to have those grandchildren and family trips, but not me. Sad and depressing, right?

I've learned that life doesn't go as I planned! In fact, I'm not anywhere near in control of it. Each of my children has their own brain and their own spirit and their own thoughts and feelings and dreams. Unfortunately, we couldn't help Trevor with his thoughts and feelings. For some reason, his path involved suicide. But that doesn't mean that I am a bad person or that I shouldn't enjoy the new reality of life with Rob and the other kids. We can still have joy in our future, even with the big hole Trevor left.

Before I started writing this book, I had this nagging thought since Trevor died that I now have an important message to share. I tried to push the thought down because the other part of my brain piped up with "Who am I to write a book? Who am I to speak to people about what we've been through? Maybe no one wants to hear it. I'm not a good enough speaker. I'm not a perfect writer. I've never published a book on Amazon before. Maybe no one will read it anyway." All these were thoughts of negativity around myself and show how little confidence I had. One of my author buddies calls this the "itty bitty shitty committee." My committee is especially skilled at always trying to keep me from living outside my comfort zone!

Learning to love and respect myself emerged from the tapping. Little by little, as I tapped away negative stuff, at the same time I reinforced that I totally loved and honored myself.

Recently I saw a video by Louise Hay, an influential motivational writer. She said if the only thing we could ever learn to do is tell ourselves in the mirror in the morning that we love and accept ourselves, then our lives would be so much better. So, I started looking at myself in the eyes in the mirror and saying, "Rebecca, I totally love you and accept you for who you are." It's quite awkward at first, but I've grown used to it now and it feels good that I love me. I have my own back.

So, loving myself has meant accepting all parts of myself: the fat on my body that has worked so hard to protect me. My bad habits of binge watching TV shows when I'm feeling tired or depressed with life. Reading true story after true story of cults and the people who have left them to help me escape my own issues. Being on edge with Rob or the kids, and losing my cool quickly in some situations. Not knowing everything I "should" know as a parent. Having high standards that I cannot even live up to.

I have worked very hard on self-forgiveness over all the awful things I feel like I've done and the thoughts I've had. It's a freeing feeling to just accept myself as the imperfect person I am, and trust that I love myself and God loves me. And that's enough.

Let me add too that when I started doing the "love myself" work, a message came through to me strong and clear. I put the following message on my vision board (which I talk about in detail in a later chapter) at the end of 2016: "Write the best, most amazing book you can, the wisest, most honest, most human book you have inside." I had no idea about when I would start writing a book or how I would do it, but I thought, "Maybe I'll start writing a book in 2017."

Basically, I've learned that loving myself is one of the hardest and most important jobs I have. I think many of us find it easier to live day to day with negative subconscious thoughts. Otherwise we have to pay attention and choose to question those thoughts that chip away at our self-esteem and make us feel guilty and unworthy. Once I chose to bring those thoughts to my conscious mind, I realized how ugly they were and how they contributed so much to my unhappiness. As I've chosen to think better thoughts and to recognize subconscious thoughts as being untrue, I've been so much more accepting of myself and others.

It's from this strong foundation of self-love that I am so equipped to love others and live my life to the fullest. And, as I'll share in the following chapter, my practice of self-love set me up to make painful but necessary changes like letting go of beliefs, habits, and people that are no longer right for me in my new life.

15.
LETTING GO, NO MORE CRAZY 8

L ETTING GO OF physical, mental, and emotional clutter and actively practicing self-love has been the hardest but most rewarding part of my journey since Trevor died. In fact, I dare to say I really didn't know how to let go of anything before Trevor died. I had this huge backpack filled over the top with past feelings, shame, and guilt that was so heavy that I needed to bend over as I walked in order to make sure I didn't topple to the ground.

I've always had this problem with moving on to a different part of life. I want to take everything from the old part and add it to the new part—every time. All the people, the stuff, the emotions.

Since Trevor died, I've had to let go of several friendships and mourn the change that happened in many of my relationships. It wasn't until I came to the understanding that those people hadn't changed—I'd changed—that I was able to forgive myself and those people for what I thought was their fault. I blamed them for not being there for me and a bunch of other things that now I consider silly or trivial. What I finally realized was that they did their very best to help however they could.

Not everyone is cut out to be 100% supportive to someone who has lost their child to suicide. Some of them want to run away, so they don't realize that it could happen to them too. Some of them just can't handle the situation of seeing their friend or family member in so much pain day in and day out, and not able to say the things that will help them. Letting go of these relationships has been one of the most painful things I've gone through alongside my grief over Trevor. How unfair that I had to lose relationships after I lost my son! For a while I thought life was so cruel.

I've had to let go of the notion that I'm supposed to know why Trevor died. I went round and round in my head on that topic for a long time: what was I supposed to learn? What are we supposed to do differently? Why are Dylan, Kendra, and Annika supposed to live with this tragedy for the rest of their lives? What should we do now?

Once I let go of the notion that I was in control of my children's lives, I realized that my path was still the same. I needed to look inside myself and find out who I am, what my purpose is here on earth, and then be patient. I know deep down with every ounce of my being that I will be reunited in Heaven with Trevor someday. Letting go of the thought that I could somehow have controlled his outcome was so freeing. There was a reason for Trevor's life, and I may never know everything I'd like to about that reason. The only thing I can do is share my story and hope it helps others.

I've already talked about letting go of clutter: physical, mental, and emotional. I'm still working on physical clutter and have come to the belief that this is a lifelong event. So much "stuff" comes into our lives on a daily basis that we have to be vigilant about letting things go that no longer serve the path we are on. The clarity from that realization has made it much easier to let go of stuff. If we carry all this extra physical stuff around that we don't even use or need anymore, then we are saddling our mind and restricting our clarity on the good we can do for others. This extra stuff leads to depression and anxiety and overwhelm.

While letting go of physical clutter, I've also let go of mental and emotional clutter. I learned from my tapping coach that mental and emotional clutter is like an onion. You start tapping on the surface stuff and then get to go deeper and deeper as you release those initial thoughts and feelings. She taught me that it is an ongoing practice for life. But, what's fascinating is that getting rid of the surface stuff and tapping into the deeper stuff is one of the most freeing experiences. It's like opening the floodgates of things that have been locked away for years and years, stuff that you may not even remember, but is still in there causing issues and limiting thoughts and beliefs in your life.

I truly released and let go of the belief that I need to keep my thoughts and feelings to myself any longer. The need to please everyone else is going by the wayside. I've lived far too many years thinking, "What will other people think?" I believe that maintaining such a concern keeps a person stuck. It has kept me stuck for years! I did not let myself unleash my inner strength and show up to my full potential because of this preoccupation. Instead I was trying to have a perfect outer image so that people would think I was a good mom, a good wife, a good Christian. That's baloney. How can I be the best mom and wife that I can be without thinking for myself, listening to my intuition, and overcoming fear to do what I'm meant to be doing? I'm serving no one when I'm not being myself.

Another thing I needed to start letting go of in order to have a better life was my body clutter. As I already explained, it was John Gabriel who directed me to start tapping because, as he explained, my body was not going to let go of the weight as long as it was still trying to protect me from the trauma of Trevor's death and the stress of my job. And it is through tapping that I'm able to let go of that body clutter.

My tapping sessions provided me the clarity that I needed in order to quit my job. That was the huge jumpstart I needed to begin to release the fat and let go of the body clutter. I came to a realization around the time I finally decided to leave my job that I had gained thirty pounds in the final two years of my time there. That really told me part of my issue was stress. And, if I could get a hold on that, then I could get a hold on losing the weight.

As of today, I have joined a program called Bright Line Eating (BLE), which is for food addictions. I have happily embraced the program and have given up sugar for the most part, more easily than I thought was possible. I am feeling fabulous about the healthy body I'm going to regain through all of 2017. I've never felt more in harmony with my food choices and my life than I feel right now.

Another thing I decluttered and released was my anger. Recently I was watching a Tony Robbins training where he talked about the "crazy 8." He showed an 8 lying on its side. Then he explained that on one side of the 8 is anger and on the other side of the 8 is depression. He said we get stuck in this crazy 8 pattern. We get really angry but can't possibly keep our energy for that anger indefinitely, so we give up and slide into depression. After a while, we get tired of being depressed, so we get motivated and angry again. He said this pattern will keep repeating until we kick ourselves out with a pattern interrupter like hope.

From this "crazy 8" explanation, I could see how my pattern worked after Trevor died. First, I was sad and depressed for long periods of time over what had happened to us and our family. Then I'd try to get myself out of the sadness and depression by getting angry that it had happened to us. But, I could only be angry for short periods of time before I'd figure nothing was going to change and our life would be like this forever, so I'd move back into the sadness and depression.

One day, I had this realization that I was in charge of changing my life. No one else could change it for me. I wish I could tell you why this realization brought such clarity to me. All I can figure is that my intuition finally became loud enough that I paid attention to her this time. I got out of the pattern by doing some major work on goals and thinking about how I might be able to help others, so I could take the focus off my negative thoughts and feelings. Once I started setting goals and coming up with ideas about how to help others, I started to feel so much excitement. I used other techniques in conjunction with the goal setting to drain away the anger and depression and resentment and frustration, thus knocking the 8 right out of the picture.

Resentment was my constant companion for a long time. I resented everyone who got to live on without having to lose their children. I resented that I couldn't have "grief time" where things were taken care of for me while I got time to figure out why this had happened and how to move forward: why couldn't I go away to a recovery facility where I didn't have to deal with people, my job, housework, my husband, my children, and just be me and try to figure out how I was going to get myself out of this terrible situation? I learned how to tap away the resentment. I accepted that God loves me no matter what, it's no one's fault that they didn't say the right words or do the right things, and it was my perception that led to my resentment. Others just did the best they could.

Letting go of the notion that I had control over my children's lives was difficult. As I already shared, I consider myself to be a logical thinker (Rob may not agree with this statement at times), so I had a deep belief that if I did A, B, and C, then my children would turn out like D. But Trevor's depression and death turned that idea on its head. Over the years of thinking this over and over, I finally have come to believe that Trevor was God's child. He was borrowed to Rob and me to raise, but God had all the power over deciding when he would take him back to Heaven. I had no control.

I felt so out of control, especially the first year after Trevor died. It was an alien feeling to me and one that was hard to get used to. Now I've finally figured out that the only thing I really can control is how I react to what's going on in my life. I only have control of my thoughts, my feelings, and my reactions to things going on around me. That's it!

Letting go of judgment—whew! That's a tough one. It's in our very nature to have to constantly judge things each day. We need to use our judgment to get dressed in the proper clothing for the day, to find something healthy to eat at each meal, and to drive without hitting things. But sometimes judgment becomes a constant nagging voice inside, criticizing the feelings or thoughts we have, or judging others who don't seem to fall in our parameters of how they "should" act.

After Trevor died, I started noticing teenagers who were dressing differently. Or I'd hear stories about silly things teenagers were doing that seemed outside the lines of what was "acceptable behavior." Instead of judging them for it, I found myself being more curious and compassionate. I thought, "I wonder why she feels the need to have pink hair? I wonder what they are feeling right now that is making them continue that type of behavior?" It was almost like my mind was in problem-solving mode. And I now have so much empathy for those in their teenage years. Life is rough when you are a teen growing up in this world. Trevor's death totally has made me see teenagers and their huge issues in a new light.

I also had to work hard to let go of my self-judgment. I was brought up in an environment that encouraged me to be a "good girl"—get good grades, obey your parents, respect your elders, say please and thank you, wear modest clothing, don't wear makeup, worry about what everyone else thinks all the time, don't show your emotions, etc. I can see that these things are nice and that my parents did the best thing they knew for helping me become a productive member of society.

But, for so many years now, I've been the ultimate judge of myself. I felt guilty for any desires I had that were outside the lines of what a "good girl" would do. I remember a friend telling me in tenth grade that "sometimes you need to let loose and have some fun!" Gosh—was I that uptight? I guess so. I was so afraid of letting teachers or my parents down that I had an extremely hard time for a while just having fun. How silly . . . The judgment of myself over my feelings and thoughts continued until after Trevor died.

When Trevor died, I was out of control in my pain. There was no way to contain the flow of tears and the feelings of helplessness and hopelessness. I wallowed instead of controlling them. When I finally decided that I could start to look into the future and live my life for the future instead of wallowing in the past, I started realizing all the major guilt I was feeling over lots of things: guilt for having publicly let myself be so sad; guilt for having this public tragedy happen in our lives; guilt over what other people must think of me as a parent now; and guilt over desiring things that maybe didn't fit into the image I had tried to create my whole entire life. Once I started working with my counselors and tapping coaches, I saw how ridiculous it was for me to judge myself and try to hide my thoughts and feelings under lock and key. In fact, that was a main issue in not being able to control my weight, being too OCD in the way I ran my household, and the difficulty I had in just letting go and having fun

I remember my last counseling session with Mary, the counselor who was helping me get clarity around my job issues at the time. She mentioned to me that I was really angry, and she wanted to see me get angry with her. She really wanted me to let go and release the anger—as I was sitting in her office.

I was stunned. I looked at her like "What are you talking about?" She kept prodding and telling me she wanted to see me get angry. And, I just couldn't do it for her. I thought, "No, I'm not angry! You've got me totally wrong."

She said what I was doing at my job was playing the nice girl and masking my anger behind a smile because that's what I had been taught to do all my life; because I judged anger as a bad thing, something to feel guilty about, so I wasn't "allowed" to show my anger. Funny thing is that I became so angry that she said that (not that I showed it to her at that moment)—I never went back to another counseling session with her. Of course, now I really appreciate everything she did for me, and I was able to update her on my progress when I saw her grocery shopping. She was happy to learn I had finally left my job and was doing much better. Thank you, Mary!

She opened my eyes to the anger that I wasn't showing publicly (my husband would laugh if he heard anyone say I didn't show anger). What she really had wanted me to do was not to go into work and be angry; she wanted me to acknowledge my anger as a real feeling and stop judging myself for it. She wanted me to release it in the proper ways and start working on ways to build more happiness. She helped me learn that bottling up my anger and not dealing with it is way worse than acknowledging it and allowing it to flow through me, so I can let it go.

I decided to start dealing with it by hiring a tapping coach. It was a scary place to go. As we started digging into all the things I was angry about, the list became very long.

Several things came out that were from years and years ago. I was carrying stuff from my growing up years. The most healing part of my work with my tapping coach was anger tapping. She allowed me to be angry and to tap all that feeling out so that I didn't blow my top in a situation at work where it wouldn't help to serve my goals. So, I'd spend every morning on my way to work yelling in my car while tapping. I look back on those commute times and giggle about what I must've looked like to others who were sitting at a stoplight. I found myself to be very expressive while letting out my anger, and I wonder if anyone else noticed. Little by little, this anger tapping opened the way to clarity in my brain. The tapping also had a side benefit of releasing feelings I wasn't necessarily focusing on. I was able to release depression, sadness, and anxiety just by tapping away my anger.

Tapping my way out of the crazy 8 cycle of anger and depression led the way to clarity about my future. Letting go has allowed me to recognize when feelings like anger start accumulating again. I've learned to be more present and allow my feelings through so that I can release them regularly. This constant letting go has provided quiet space, which has given my inner voice strength. Once my true voice started showing up more regularly, I started to listen and let myself be guided. It's been a transformative process that I am sharing in the next chapter.

16.
LISTENING TO THE SMART COOKIE

I OFTEN JOKE with people now that maybe if I would've listened to myself during my college years I may have become a flamenco dancer! I recently got that idea from a fellow business friend who runs a successful flamenco studio in California and also teaches online. I mention Rina here because I am so inspired by how she unleashes herself to the world through dance every day. It's her absolute passion, and she gets to pass it on to others in a big way.

That's what I want to do—pass on my passion to others in a big way every day. I'm not talking about flamenco dancing, but finding my inner power and passion, and passing it on to the world. I'm really sad that it took a tragedy like losing Trevor to suicide to wake me up from a life that was going just "like it's supposed to go" with no real fulfillment for myself.

Yes, I love my family and my children. They provide great fulfillment, but there's always been a piece missing. I've heard this voice for years telling me there's something more out there. It's hard to explain the feeling if you've never felt it. I've searched and read many books, listened to many talks, gone to conferences, and talked with others to discover that missing piece. And now I've finally figured it out. The missing piece is joy and fulfillment in the work that I do, and a key to tapping into that is listening to my intuition.

This led me to the decision to leave my 25-year accounting career. What I truly enjoyed about accounting jobs was coming up with processes and systems to help organize the business-side of an organization. The achiever in me loves taking something from messy to neat. There's a lot of fulfillment for me in that process. But, what I noticed is that after the initial part of cleaning up the mess is complete, I lose interest in the ongoing day-to-day maintenance of the system.

At one point a couple of years ago, I thought I was supposed to be a professional organizer. I even tried it out with one client. In many respects it was a cathartic experience for both of us. While we were organizing her home, we were talking about our lives. I could see how she was beginning to see her life would be changed for the better when she let go of her physical clutter.

But, my bigger aha moment was realizing that people also need to let go of their mental clutter. I believe our outer world reflects what's going on inside. Possibly the first work that needs to be done is gaining mental clarity about where you want to go in life.

That's the work I will be doing from now on—starting with this book! I gained this clarity because I've done my own work, reading, and research on mindset, goal setting, and achieving peace, and I have started to use other tools in my life that have helped me find my greater purpose. I have started listening intently to my intuition and have to admit that she's a smart cookie.

I'm sorry I haven't necessarily given her my ear before this. But, I'm in tune now. She has told me that my life's work is to help others dig out from underneath the mental and physical clutter, so they can reveal their true purpose and calling on this earth. They can also find the work that gives them joy and fulfillment, the work that they are uniquely qualified to do. I am truly excited by the thought that I can help other women clarify this for themselves.

The clarity and ability to get in tune with my intuition that I gained when I did the tapping and decluttering work led me to question the current job situation I was in: "Why am I doing a job that makes me so angry and feel so unappreciated? Why am I allowing other people to walk all over me? Why am I allowing other people's thoughts about what I should or shouldn't do control my life?" I became so sad that I had not stuck up for myself; that I had gotten into a situation that I felt was unwinnable for me; and that I had let myself stay somewhere mostly out of the fear that I'd lose a "good job" or "good benefits" if I quit.

In the end, it really was all up to me the whole time. I had let myself be the victim for a good while, so I wouldn't have to accept the failure as my failure. Not anyone else's failure. The failure I felt was that I couldn't make the job be what it should be. That I couldn't make the organization run the way that made the most business sense. That I couldn't find a way to be happier in that position. I initially loved pouring the blame for all that on other people.

What a wake-up call when I finally realized it really is up to me: it was my decision to stay or go. It was my decision on what my thoughts and feelings were while I was there. It was always up to me. I just allowed myself to wallow in the indulgent belief that my life was miserable because of the circumstances I found myself in at the job. Looking back, I'm guessing I received a lot of attention by being in the victim role. Maybe I felt there wasn't enough support and attention given after Trevor died, so this was another way to get it. Admittedly, it sounds ridiculously manipulative from my current perspective, but I also know that grief is its own animal. At the time, I was doing the best I could. And I accept and love myself in all my imperfection.

My mentor Fabienne Fredrickson says, "After the breakdown, the breakthrough is right around the corner." I know the breakthrough I'm having now is worth the years of pain and confusion. I have found the clarity and the voice of my inner self through the decluttering work I've engaged in to alleviate that pain and confusion. And, I wouldn't have been forced to do the decluttering work on myself and make the tough decisions I needed to make if everything had been going just a little bit better. If I had been thrown just one or two bones during that final year in my job, I wouldn't have had the opportunity to confront myself and step out of my comfort zone to finally hear my inner voice and become the person I am meant to be.

Writing this brings tears to my eyes. I am so grateful now for everything I've gone through to get to this point. None of it is wasted. All of it is so valuable in becoming the best me. I feel grateful for this chance that I've been given now to break out of anything I ever thought I "had to" be or "had to" do. I feel so grateful that I'm allowing myself to finally listen to my inner voice and express who I truly am.

My self-esteem was at an all-time low by the time I finally listened to my intuition and then gave myself permission to stand up for myself, put boundaries in place, and give notice at my job. That was the first time in a long time I felt new hope for my life—when I could finally say, "Enough is enough," and let everyone know that I was unwilling anymore to stay and take the garbage I thought that they were pouring on me. Turns out I was pouring it all over myself. It was a major victory for me to walk out the door and never look back.

Since I've quit that job and been able to listen to and honor my intuition, I've had some amazing self-discoveries. I've started to question lots of stuff I thought I "should" be doing. "Why do I say yes to everything? Why do I do others' bidding even when it doesn't serve my highest good, which eventually leads to the highest good for my family?" I started trying something new. I started trying to say no when I felt like what was being asked of me didn't fit in with how I determined I wanted to live my life. It's been a painful process of stepping out of the box I had placed myself in.

And, as expected, I got pushback. I remember when I decided that being the auditor for our church books was something I just couldn't fit into my schedule anymore, as I was always given the stuff at the very last minute and expected to crank it out and give my blessing. I honored myself by telling the treasurer of the church that I wouldn't be doing the audit that year or in the future.

I had three or four people try to get me to continue doing it that year. And I stuck to my boundary. I kindly and politely kept saying no. One person responded, "You can't just quit," and gave me some story about what was going on in their life. I was horrified to find that my anger came spouting out the top, and I literally yelled a response. I needed to take responsibility again for my anger and recognize that others' thoughts or feelings about me were not my problem.

I was so tired by that time of doing things others thought I should do. I was just at the beginning journey of standing up for myself and it wasn't going well. It was another clue as to why I usually didn't push back or say no to things: because if I said no, people might think bad things about me or not like me anymore.

Regardless of the pushback, I was proud of myself for giving that thing up. I decided to try saying no to more things. For example, I started saying no to doing tax returns that weren't in my zone of genius. Because I'm a CPA, people thought I must be a tax expert when in fact my expertise was in accounting systems. I never liked doing taxes, and I'm not particularly practiced in that area. I even have a difficult time getting myself to do my own!

Then there's the small things my intuition guided me to stop doing. For example, I was always accommodating to others even when they consistently wanted to change dates and times on plans that we had made. I decided I would no longer be so accommodating and flexible. In fact, now if someone wants to meet with me for lunch, but then they keep changing the date and time, I politely end the expectation that we are having the lunch together. It was hard the first couple of times.

I sometimes wondered to myself why I attracted so many friends who were wishy-washy, the kind that say they want to hang out, but something always comes up at the last minute and they call and cancel or reschedule. With these types of friends I'd find myself bitter and resentful about the fact that I seemed to be the one who wanted our friendship more, so I'd hang on and let them reschedule as many times as they wanted. Somehow I thought that was helping our friendship out. Really, what it was doing was not honoring my feelings and boundaries. So, I now honor myself by listening to my intuition. If something comes up last minute and I don't feel like rescheduling, then I say that it's not going to work out.

That goes with my schedule at home too. I'm honoring my boundaries around my work time in building my business from home. I'm not one who likes lots of flexibility and unknowns, and I've decided that that's OK with me. I feel safest when I know what the schedule is and can plan ahead.

When Rob decides last minute to drive out of town to visit family or friends, I check in with myself about whether it's something I really want to do at the time. If not, I say no, and I feel OK with it. I used to let a big guilt trip hang over my head if I had the desire to say no. Now, I've gotten better and better at listening to my intuition, saying no if I don't want to do something, and letting it go.

Obviously, there are times when I'm totally happy to say yes. Of course I want to spend time with Rob, and there are times too when I feel a need for a break from a project I'm working on. I'm not 100% unavailable for surprise dates or trips but just more thoughtful about what I feel at the time. I've tuned into my intuition, and it's doing wonders in my life.

As I'm finishing this chapter, I'm wondering if some of you are thinking that all this "listening to my intuition" stuff makes me sound self-centered and greedy. Initially, that's one of the fears I had about expressing myself and my feelings. I had thought that others wouldn't like me or would think I was a bad person. But, after much reading and thought on it, I've come to recognize that I cannot be fully there for my family and friends and clients if I'm not fulfilled myself. If I don't recharge my batteries, have "me time," and protect my boundaries around my time and feelings, then I will not be able to fully show up as my best and truest self. And, I believe that showing up fully as myself will be the best for my family, the best for my business, the best for my writing, and the best for any other relationships I choose to be a part of.

Knowing that I have the choice of how I allow myself to be treated gives me back my power. Instead of feeling weak and powerless and the victim of circumstances, I feel strong and confident and hopeful. This intuitive me is now available to create the life and future I want. I am in charge of creating that—no one else can do it for me. A valuable tool I used to help me create that purposeful life and future is a dream board, which I discuss in the next chapter.

17.
POWERFUL PICTORIAL

A T THE END of December 2016 I decided to put together a dream board. A dream board, also called a vision board, is a pictorial of things you want to show up in your life, and it includes anything—vacations, relationships, or the type of home or car you want.

Here's how making a dream board works. You spend time thinking about your goals and dreams, and then you create a physical representation of them on the dream board. You look at it and connect with those dreams on a daily basis. It's a way to link the small choices and actions of your daily life to your greater life dreams; it helps you sync the two.

I've created dream boards a couple of times in the past with poster board and cut-up magazines. This time I did one on the computer and saved part of it as my screensaver. I put pictures on there of my business's money goal, changes I wanted to make in my master bedroom, the foods I wanted to grow to love (lots of colorful fruits and veggies), a picture of a flat tummy, travel destinations, and a quote about the book I wanted to write.

Now, every time I open my computer, I look at my dream board. It's a welcomed reminder about my life goals and what I'm working towards.

I can't believe the power of my dream board. Here are two amazing things that I've manifested since putting them on my dream board:

1. Writing this book

2. Overcoming my sugar addiction

Book

Here's the quote I put on my dream board about the book I wanted to write: "Write the best, most amazing book you can, the wisest, most honest, most human book you have inside." I don't know who originally wrote this quote; I found it on Pinterest and clipped it to my dream board because it spoke to me about what I aimed to do with my first book.

I've been wanting to write a book for decades. Ever since I was a kid I thought it would be amazing to be an author. Books have always been a huge part of my life. I had never put this goal on a dream board before since my idea of what it took to write a book was that you had to slave over a rough draft for three years and try endlessly to get a publisher for it. It seemed impossible for a nonprofessional writer like me, but I put this goal on my dream board anyway, thinking, "Maybe I'll actually start a book this year."

I didn't have any idea of how I'd start a book or maybe even fully what I would write about. I thought I wanted to write something about Trevor's death, but I just wasn't sure how to go about it. Once I put it on my dream board, things showed up for me. I belong to this amazing Voxer group of six female online business owners. We support each other in growing our businesses and share the ups and downs of the entrepreneurial journey. I told them about my desire to write a book and showed them that it was on my dream board.

One day, one of the members of my Voxer group emailed me to say she had received notice of a program that teaches people how to self-publish a book, and she recommended that I check it out. Self-publishing wasn't new to me. Over the years I had read blogs about self-publishing and had noticed some people were having massive success with it.

At my group members' suggestion, I attended a webinar about the program and learned about its step-by-step system from finding the idea for your book to launching it. This particular program spoke to me in a way no other self-publishing blog had before. It didn't take long to sign up (see information about the self-publishing program at the end of my book).

Within a few days of enrolling, I had totally changed the paradigm about what it would take to write a book: wow! I could have my book written, edited, and launched for sale on Amazon within 90 days—incredible!

What I learned: things happen much faster than you'd think when they are on your dream board. I had been thinking I'd just "start a book" in 2017. Instead, I clarified my topic, wrote a rough draft of 34,000 words, and you are seeing the final result of that process. All within about 90 days!

As I'm writing this, I think how unbelievable it is that you can write and self-publish a book within six months. I took that as God saying, "Go for it! I want you to share this message," so I listened to my intuition right away, enrolled in the self-publishing course, and followed every single step to a T. I am so grateful for this. It showed me that I can do it, and I can be successful at it—especially when I listen to my intuition. I feel so much pride about having the "stick-to-it-ness" attitude of just trusting the process and going for it.

I wonder if I'd ever have done it without my dream board . . .

Sugar Addiction

I've always wondered, "Can I ever truly be 'happy, thin, and free' [a phrase from Susan Pierce Thompson and her Bright

Line Eating program]?" I ended up writing this phrase—
"happy, thin, and free"—as well as some others and posting it
on my dream board along with some enticing pictures of
healthy food and healthy bodies.

After putting this on my dream board, I had absolutely no idea
how I'd achieve it—overcoming the sugar addiction—during
2017. I had tried many things in the past, and none led to long-
term physical and mental health. But, I believe that what you
put on your dream board will manifest, so I put it there
anyway.

One of my business mentors sent along an email to talk about a
program she had been through in 2016 that changed the way
she looks at food. I checked it out—and was immediately
drawn to it. The founder of Bright Line Eating (BLE) is a
fellow food addict, and she has totally been free of sugar for
more than 10 years. Once again, this was a paradigm shift for
me: someone as addicted to sugar as I am can be free of it, lose
all the excess weight, and live in a healthy-sized body the rest
of her life? Wow—I had to see this.

I connected with someone who had blogged about the topic,
and she gave me the main principles of the program. I started
immediately putting them into place. I decided that I'd try to
eat the way the program taught to prove to myself I was serious
before investing any money in it and officially enrolling. After
proving that I could eat the BLE way, I went ahead and joined
the program, so I could learn all the tips and get all the support
I needed to make it a permanent part of my life. Part of me was
still uncertain that I really could make an everlasting change in
this area of my life. I'd tried so many times before.

I didn't know what was different this time, but amazingly
enough, at this writing I've been free of sugar for over 100
days and have lost over 20 pounds. The pounds are not the
biggest win for me. The freedom from thinking about food
from the time I get up in the morning to the time I go to bed at

night is the best part of what I've learned thus far in this Bright Line Eating journey. I know that this is the foundational change I needed to make in my life to make every other area work better. Freedom from sugar (about 95% of the time) has provided me with greater clarity and time to work on all kinds of other things instead of worrying about when I'll get that next piece of chocolate.

Creating the dream board and connecting with it multiple times each day has provided me with welcomed reminders of some of my bigger goals. When my mind is swimming with my day's to-do list, the dream board on my computer screen gently connects me to those bigger goals such that seemingly I've found myself well underway to their achievement.

Next we'll explore goal setting and how it sets you up to more readily take possibilities from your dream board and make them into realities in your life.

18.
PURPOSEFUL GOAL SETTING

WHILE I'VE PRACTICED goal setting over the course of my life and found satisfaction in doing so, it's only since Trevor died that I've realized how truly powerful it can be for my mental health and for finding joy. While any kind of goal setting can be helpful, like my initial applications of it, since I've refined my understanding and practice of it, I've benefitted from it much more profoundly than I had before.

Goal Setting Initially for Me

Here are some things I accomplished using goal setting in the more distant past:

1. Passed the four-part CPA exam on the first try (this was back when you were only allowed to take all 4 parts at once!).

2. Swam the 2.25-mile Teal Lake Swim (after about a 20-year break from competitive swimming) and finished in the top half of the 100 or so participants.

3. Was in the best shape of my life after completing 6 months of the "Body for Life" program before my husband and I went on a 10-year anniversary trip to Puerto Vallarta.

There are more things too that I accomplished due to goal setting, but these stick out as big accomplishments to me.

One thing I notice about these big accomplishments is that they didn't stick around to change my life. Each was a discrete goal and an end in itself; each didn't have longer-lasting follow-through. That's the difference between the goal setting I've been doing since Trevor died and how I practiced goal setting before.

More Recent Goal Setting

The goal setting I now engage in is much more purposeful. I'm careful in creating my goals because I don't want to spend my time working towards something that is an end in itself. I am careful to set goals that carry through and lead to more possibilities through their accomplishment. I'll show what I mean with an example.

My first very intentional goal was to start an online coaching business. It's the goal I focused on when I quit my job, and it was enough to bring me out of my negative mojo.

I determined that an online business would be satisfying to me on a number of levels. For example, one of my top five strengths, according to Tom Rath's Strengthsfinder 2.0 is "Learner." Another one is "Achiever." In building an online business, there's a constant list of stuff to learn and achieve: set up a website, write blog posts, make screenshot videos, get set up on social media, set up a membership area to protect paid content, learn to use an email delivery system, learn to create images, etc.

The learner in me just loves it. And the achiever in me likes to check boxes off that things are done.

Every day at the end of the day I really feel like I achieved something that is working towards helping a lot of people. So, in this way, I am making progress towards achieving a goal that will have tremendous follow-through and impact.

Establishing my own coaching business, in which I provide support to other people, is a goal that doesn't end once it is achieved; in fact, its impact will only grow and positively influence more and more people as time goes on. These are the kind of goals I'm now interested in working towards: multi-dimensional goals that have compounding effects in their achievement.

I've also set some life goals.

I was in so much misery and disarray from losing Trevor and from working in a job that took up a lot of mental and emotional energy. I felt like I was just living life as it was randomly being thrown at me. I was at the will of anything.

There was no focus for my life. I said it many times to Rob, "What is our focus? Where are we heading?" And, I got really frustrated sometimes that he wouldn't figure that out for me. Once I quit my job, I felt I had the mental energy to figure it out for myself. No one else can figure out what your goals are for yourself. You must do it!

With this in mind and with Rob's support we set the goal of living in new places during the winter parts of the year. I let go of the limiting belief that you have to wait until you are 62 to "retire" and live in Florida, Texas, South Carolina, or other such warm places for the winter. I have let go of the self-doubt I have in my ability to create a business that's location independent and that can support our goals and dreams. So, my goal is not only to establish an online business but to live a multi-location lifestyle with my family.

Notice how this second goal complements the first goal, rather than standing alone. Notice how this second goal—living in multiple locations—will also compound on itself, opening my and my family's possibilities for new friendships, languages, cultures, cuisines, etc., all of which can lead to even more possibilities. It's a goal that isn't an end in itself but a beginning to so many more possibilities of joy.

In my exploration of goal setting and goal manifestation, I've encountered the important work of Dr. Paul Scheele who teaches the following seven steps to goal setting:

1. Clarity

2. Visualization

3. Acceptance

4. Focus

5. Intuition

6. Action

7. Manifestation

To understand how these seven steps work, I will share how I've explored my personal goals using them.

Clarity

I've heard the question many times around goal setting: "If you don't know where you're going, how are you possibly going to end up there?" When I talk about clarity, I don't mean you just need to write down a list of goals. Instead they should be SMART goals. I don't know who came up with the notion of SMART, but I've seen it around goal setting in different books and teachings. SMART goals refer to goals that are *specific, measurable, attainable, reasonable,* and *time sensitive.*

What I find works well is using my dream board for the general idea of what I want with each of my goals. Then, I use my journal to add more specificity and clarity to each goal, and I apply the SMART guidelines if it's feasible.

Denise Duffield Thomas, a money mindset coach, advises recording your goals as if you are writing a letter to Santa and making sure to be very specific. She also suggests using the be-do-have exercise on a regular basis. This is really a fun one. It's about doing a brain dump related to who you want to *be* in life, what you want to *do* in life, and what you want to *have* in life. Then, take those lists and cull them down to the top detailed goals that are the most important. Sometimes, looking at your final be-do-have findings can clarify the several top goals that would make all the other goals come true. Those top goals are the ones that I write in clear detail in my journal.

Visualization

I remember reading Michael Phelps' book *No Limits: The Will to Succeed* several years ago. What struck me as fascinating is that he would set an exact time goal of when he'd hit the wall in his races. He would visualize over and over again his race and coming in at that exact time. So, I've been using this visualization practice around my goals too.

When I visualize my goals, I close my eyes in a quiet space and feel what it would feel like to be living my goals already. I notice what's going on in my day and around me if I'm already living the life I desire, running the business I want, and living in the place I want.

Once you visualize what you feel like and what things look like, Paul Scheele advises you to (1) write it down in detail in your journal, (2) read it daily, (3) visualize it again with feeling, and (4) write down any new details that come from that exercise. This is actually quite fun to do.

I like to do this mindset visualization practice right away in the morning. It's a nice way to wake up to the day with a positive attitude about where I am headed, and it helps me focus on what needs to be done to get there.

Another part of goal setting at this visualization stage that Denise Duffield Thomas talks about is decluttering. She says to look around and determine what things would come along with you in the next phase of your life. Since I love decluttering so much anyway, I've tried to use it in this visualization form she describes. Let me explain:

As I've already shared, Rob and I set a big goal that complements my goal of starting an online business: we want to travel and go to warmer places in the winter.

Having jobs that allow for a few weeks of vacation a year just doesn't give us enough time away from the cold, snowy weather of Upper Michigan between January and May. But, we've determined that our real goal is to be able to live six months in Upper Michigan and six months in a warmer climate. This is something we want to happen as soon as our youngest daughter, Annika, graduates from high school in 2021. That is a clear goal to which I can apply decluttering, visualization, and journaling.

Decluttering, in the case of this goal, means thinking about what we'd actually need and want to live that life. Would we want to own our current large home? If so, would we want to rent it out while we are away? What about all the stuff that's in it? Would it serve our life in the best way to have a bunch of extra stuff sitting around, especially if we only live in Upper Michigan in the summer? I'm thinking not.

I visualize us decluttering the winter clothes and winter sports items. We'll also declutter all the stuff that has sat around for ten years or more and not been looked at. Moving back and forth every six months certainly isn't a life that allows us to pack a bunch of stuff to haul around each time we move. We are still in the middle of creating the vision for that life goal, and I'm excited for the literal decluttering phase to occur!

Sometimes, during visualizations, writing down goals, and reading goals to myself, thoughts come up like "That takes a lot of work" or "We can't afford to do that" or "I'll never be able to make that much money." Dr. Paul Scheele encourages you to write these worries in your journal. He teaches that these are blocks that stand in your way of manifesting your goals.

To handle these blocks, I write them down each time they pop up when I read and visualize my goals. Next I read each block I've written and turn it into a positive statement. I then use EFT tapping to clear that block from my thinking. I may have to do tapping on the same block when it comes up on another day, especially if it's a worry or fear that has stuck with me since my childhood.

Related to the visualization stage is something Denise Duffield Thomas calls "upgrades," a notion I really love. The idea is to write down things in your life that wouldn't fit into the future vision you have for yourself. For instance, what kind of clothing are you wearing on your future self who has achieved her goals? What kind of space do you live in? What kind of relationships do you have? What kind of foods do you eat? What kinds of things surround you in your home?

Denise suggests recording the things that need to be "upgraded" in your life. Next, you start slowly to upgrade these things. This means you choose certain small things in your current life to upgrade (as in, change for the better), so you are consistently working to step into the new life you are seeking to live. One easy thing for me is to get rid of clothes that don't fit anymore. I will not be bringing tons of old, non-fitting clothing into a new life where I'm "happy, thin, and free."

Acceptance

The next part of goal setting has to do with becoming OK with wanting more, as well as accepting that we are capable of having anything we want in this life. We are capable of fabulous relationships, perfect health, a peaceful existence, and living where and how we want to live. This involves working on what we think is possible for ourselves. Our limiting beliefs keep us stuck inside a box of possibilities that sometimes is so hard to see outside of, so these self-imposed limits are something we must be aware of and actively refuse to believe in.

Part of the practical things I've done to expand my mind into the realm of what's possible is to read success stories. I love rags-to-riches or personal empowerment stories of weight loss and health gain by someone who had literally been heavy their whole life. The common thread in all the success stories is mindset. Sure, there are a lot of actions that took place to come to the successful outcome, but it all started with the person changing their mindset of what's possible.

Many times we can't see what's possible until someone else has done it and showed us it's possible. I always remember the 4-minute mile story. Sir Roger Bannister broke the 4-minute mile mark in 1954 when no one else thought it was remotely possible. Amazingly enough, within the next 4 years, a number of people started breaking the 4-minute mile mark. Once the mindset changed about what was possible, more runners began breaking the 4-minute mile mark.

Even though I've never personally made the income level that I have a goal for right now for my business, I realize that it doesn't mean it's not possible. I read successful business stories all the time that help to reframe the negative thinking I have. Sometimes I write income goals on sticky notes and stick them in weird places like the side of the nightstand, the mirror in my bathroom, the inside of my closet, and the screen of my computer. It's just a tool to help my subconscious get on board with the number, so I don't think it's so far out of the realm of possibility.

Acceptance also means accepting ourselves to be the imperfect beings we already are and loving ourselves for exactly who we are at the moment. If we strip away all the past things that have happened and all the future things we fear or are anxious about, then right now is what we have. And, if you are sitting here reading this, you are perfectly fine in this moment. Just as I am perfectly fine and have everything I need in the moment I am writing this.

Living in the past or in the future really screws up the peaceful feelings we have about the moment we are in. We can be triggered subconsciously at any moment by something we see that reminds us of a past event that happened, and instantly our body remembers how we usually react to that past thing. That brings up those feelings again: remorse, guilt, anger, resentment, hatred. Or we could start worrying about things in the future that we have no evidence are going to happen: I'm going to get cancer or my daughter might die in a car accident or my husband might have a heart attack. If we spend our present moment worrying about future things, we are victims again to our own thoughts.

Byron Katie wrote a book titled *Love What Is*. From the title alone I can already see what a tremendous gift I can have from myself if I look at myself as I am now and my life exactly as it is now—and just "love what is." I can love all the past events and not put any judgment on them. I can just love that they were the path my life took, and that's it. There's no need to judge them right or wrong, good or bad. Why do I know things were meant to happen exactly as they did? Because they happened. There's no changing that.

Right now, I can love myself for all my flaws: my quickness to get impatient, my excess fat, my lingering self-doubts, my guilt over things I've done or thought, etc. I can love my house right now for exactly what it is, my car for exactly what it is, my marriage for all its imperfectness, my business for not being at its potential, and everything else in my life that's exactly as it should be at this moment. I don't need to think about the future. I just need to love what is right now. Imagine if you do that too—love everything in all its imperfectness.

What clarity it will create for us to be able to embrace ourselves and our lives for what they are at this moment, and still it is OK to want to move in a direction towards something different. (Even as I'm writing this, I feel some anxiety about the whole "love what is" notion, so I'm embracing that tinge of anxiety as an OK feeling—no judgment.)

Focus

Turning our attention to what we want is the whole process of focus—not focusing on what we don't want. So, in our day-to-day existence if we look around when we get out of bed in the morning and start focusing on all the stuff that doesn't fit with the goal we have of our future self, then that's the stuff that's going to come into our lives more and more—the stuff we don't want. It takes effort to do the opposite and focus on what we want, but it's worth the care it takes.

So many things really are beyond our control, and we must love what is. For instance, when I get out of bed in the morning and see another gray, snowy, blizzard-looking day in the middle of March, my habit is to think, "Snow again! When is this ever going to end? Are we even going to have spring this year?" But, since that starts a train of negatives and looking for the negatives around me, I have learned to (most of the time) catch that thought and instead say, "What a precious day I've been given to work on my goals again. Boy that snow sure is beautiful when it clings to the trees like that."

Now, if I'm being frank, Rob has told me many times over the years that I tend to look at the negatives in life. My counselor pointed out once that because of my profession (as an auditor and CPA), much of my job is spent looking for errors, mistakes, and things that are wrong, so they can be fixed to make a system more efficient. She felt I had a hard time separating that type of work from the prevailing attitude in my brain. Her observation made sense to me, so I've been working really hard to change that habit.

One thing that helps me is doing a short journaling exercise that makes me think of one thing I'm grateful for. Gratefulness leaves no room for negative thinking. Another helpful thing Rob has said in the past is "Let's find solutions, not problems" (typical engineer thinking!). My morning routine is set up to do mindset work to focus more on the positives of achieving my goals.

If you haven't read *The Miracle Morning* by Hal Elrod, I highly suggest it. Hal talks about starting out your day with "me time." In other words, work on stuff that's important to you before going about and attending to others' needs. He suggests doing things that are important for both your mental and physical health. Most of *The Miracle Morning* is based around mental health.

After I first read the book, I set up a morning around the following: 10 minutes of guided meditation, 10 minutes of visualization, 10 minutes of affirmations, 10 minutes of journaling, and 20 minutes of reading something inspirational. Since then, I have different iterations of the miracle morning depending on what I want to focus on. Lately my miracle morning is about guided meditation, reviewing my goals, and journaling.

Focusing also means deciding what should stay or go in your life in order to work towards your goals. And, figuring out which two to three large goals you want to work on this year. Right now, my three large goals revolve around getting this book published, releasing body fat, and building a business that will allow for the "snow bird" lifestyle Rob and I want to live. Those are three hugely amazing goals that I know will have such a positive impact on my life.

In determining the three goals I am focusing on, I can build habits around those goals. For example, for my goal of losing the excess fat, I have simplified Bright Line Eating down to its most basic form and then formed habits from there. BLE's simplest form is its four basic rules: no sugar, no flour, eat only three meals per day, and weigh all my food. Once I found seven to ten meals that are absolutely delicious, and three to five local restaurants with one meal I can make work into my plan, I'm totally satisfied and don't at all feel I'm missing out on anything. I made a promise to myself that I would make BLE the simplest it can be, so I don't get exhausted with cooking. And my approach is working.

So, I'm taking my BLE approach and trying to fit it into my business-building experience. I'm trying to clarify just three to four "rules" and then build habits around those, so I can be successful in my business too.

Intuition

I've mentioned intuition and its significance in my life in some depth already in this book, so rather than revisiting that journey, we'll concentrate on the relationship between intuition and goal setting.

Paul Scheele gives several different mindset exercises in his "Abundance for Life" course to help people connect with their intuition and then apply their intuition to goal setting. He says certain mindset practices help us to tune the nervous system so that we can more readily get in touch with our inner wisdom and intuition.

When you do mindset work and you enter a meditative state, you can then present your big goal to your inner self. Then you can ask that true and pure part of yourself, "What's the next step I need to take to reach this goal?" and your inner self can present you with the most insightful response. Your inner self isn't plagued by mind chatter, worry, pride, or doubt. It will give you the support you seek if you take the time and give it the quiet space it needs to be heard.

I've just started working on this and am excited to get to know my inner guide and intuition on a whole new level.

Action

Funny thing about action—I've learned that action should never be the most important part about goal setting. For instance, if we decide we want to take a trip to Hawaii, and we immediately go into action and pack our suitcases and get in the car to go to the airport, how would that trip turn out?

The results of immediate action:

Clarity—There's no clarity. For instance, where do we want to go in Hawaii? How do we want to get there? What things do we want to see? What do we need to pack? How long are we going to be gone?

Visualization—There's no visualization. Taking quiet time to close our eyes and feel what it will feel like to be in Hawaii, and see some of the things we think we may want to do when we are there—this will help manifest the trip for us. And it will help us manifest the type of trip we want. Is it sightseeing or lying on the beach? Is it climbing a volcano or getting a history lesson?

Acceptance—There's no acceptance. In other words, what are the limiting thoughts and beliefs we have that could crop up and make the trip not go as we planned? For instance, "It's too expensive. We have to be gone so long, so who's going to take care of our regular life (the dog and Annika) while we are away?" These are the lists of things that need to be dealt with, so we can turn them into positive, solutions-oriented statements of acceptance.

Focus—If we started with clarity and wrote down all the things we want to happen in our Hawaii trip, we'd be able to visualize those things and focus beforehand on how fantastic the trip is going to be, all the benefits and great feelings we will have while we are on the trip, and how easily our life will be managed while we are gone and when we return. By focusing this way, we continue to manifest a beautiful trip that has no hassles and fulfills all the things we want it to be about. It's a way to concentrate on the positives in order to get the most enjoyment out of the trip.

Intuition—Finally, if we pay attention to our intuition while going through the planning and manifesting process, we will gain insights into how to make the trip better and how to have the most fulfilling experience in the planning phase, travelling phase, and have everything taken care of as needed while we are away.

Only after we've done all those steps is it time to take action. We now get to plan the dates, buy the tickets, search for hotels. I sincerely believe that by getting clarity around what we truly want and then visualizing it, then we are best positioned for it happen in the way that most parallels our wants and needs. I've heard it said that the universe will conspire to give us what we want when we become extremely clear on what it is we do want.

A fabulous story about manifesting the trip of a lifetime can be found in my money mindset mentor Denise Duffield-Thomas' book *Lucky Bitch*. Amazingly by deliberately manifesting their goals for travel beforehand, she and her husband ended up "working" a six-month dream job consisting of staying in five-star honeymoon resorts around the world and documenting their experience. That book made a manifesting believer out of me!

So, to wrap it up, here are the steps, as taught by Paul Scheele, to manifest goals in our lives:

- Clarity
- Visualization
- Acceptance
- Focus
- Intuition
- Action and Manifestation

These goal setting and mindset steps helped me to extricate myself from the cycle of sadness, anger, resentment, and depression. These steps give me an invaluable framework through which I can process my goals in order to achieve more profound outcomes. I don't have the time or space to focus on negatives. I am confident you'll find the same.

19.

AN AMAZING PEACE

THIS JOURNEY HAS been hard. It's been wrought with ups and downs, twists and turns. Just when I thought I was feeling better, something would come back up and push me into the hole of despair, hopelessness, and depression again.

Why would God take Trevor and leave me here? I couldn't really ponder that question while working at a job that was draining me mentally and emotionally every day.

Once I decided to leave that job, the real healing in my life began. I started to acknowledge my true inner desires and find out what I needed to fill myself up, so I could show up in a better way for myself, my family, and my friends.

I started listening to my intuition again. Boy, that inner me had been pushed way down, and now I had let her out. She had a lot of things to tell me, and I'm so happy that I'm now paying attention to her.

If I hadn't started listening to my intuition, I would still not be sleeping peacefully and soundly, I'd still be stuffing my face with food to fill some empty place inside, I would not have found the resources to write this book, and I would not be on my way to building the thriving coaching business I know in my heart and soul is what I'm supposed to be here for.

I feel sad that Trevor had to die in order for me to pay attention to my life and purpose, and to realize that trudging through days without any bigger purpose and bigger goals in life is dying, not living.

I feel sad that I couldn't show up in this way for Trevor, the way that I'm showing up for myself now. But, I know I can feel sad about it. I just don't have to feel guilty and angry and beat myself up about it anymore.

I feel an amazing peace now about what life is about and what I'm here to do. I feel peace that Trevor is in a beautiful place, but he left such a wonderful mark on our lives. And we will never forget that. I feel peace that I can look at Trevor's baby pictures and remember what a happy, chubby, smiley, loving soul he was.

The way he died does not define the way he lived and the joy he brought to our lives. His life and death have taught me so much, and I'm forever grateful that I had the opportunity to be his mom for the short time he was here on this earth. What an honor and privilege that was.

In some weird way I feel blessed that I have been able to take this tragedy and use it to wake me up to the fact that every one of us should be living for today. We shouldn't be hanging onto old habits that aren't serving us. We should be looking to big goals for our future and realize that to reach those goals we need to let go of lots of negative stuff from our past. Trevor would want that and I believe he'd be proud of the changes I've made in my life. I think of him as a quiet cheerleader who is cheering me on to achieve things that he may have wanted to achieve for his life. I live through and for him.

I hope you are able to take the lessons I've learned from this tragedy and apply some or all of them to your life.

Are you living your best, authentic life? Are you fulfilling the purpose you are here on earth for? Are you listening to your inner voice?

My goal in life now is to love openly, live authentically, joyfully fill my life's purpose, and teach others to do the same.

Thank you. I'm honored you stayed with me through this retelling of my journey to peace.

RESOURCES

Books

- *Bright Line Eating: The Science of Living Happy, Thin and Free* by Susan Pierce Thompson, PhD

- *Embrace Your Magnificence* by Fabienne Fredrickson

- *The Forgotten Mourners: Sibling Survivors of Suicide* by John's Sister

- *Lucky Bitch* by Denise Duffield Thomas

- *The Miracle Morning: The Not-So-Obvious Secret Guaranteed to Transform Your Life (Before 8 AM)* by Hal Elrod

- *A Mother's Reckoning* by Sue Klebold

- *No Time to Say Goodbye* by Carla Fine

Courses and Programs

- Abundance for Life Course created by Paul Scheele: learningstrategies.com/AbundanceForLife/Home.asp

- National Alliance for Mental Illness Family to Family Program: nami.org

- Self-Publishing School: visit http://bit.ly/2pxP3uo for more information

Organizations

- The American Foundation for Suicide Prevention: afsp.org

- The Compassionate Friends: compassionatefriends.org

Other

- EFT and Tapping: see Brad Yates on YouTube or go to youtube.com/user/eftwizard

- National Suicide Prevention Lifeline: 1-800-273-8255

Acknowledgments

To the Ishpeming-Negaunee bowling team, the NHS golf team, and Trevor's amazing classmates and friends—thank you so much for the hugs and for inviting us to be a part of your lives during these tough years. I've enjoyed watching your band concerts, musicals, bowling meets, and graduations. I hope each and every one of you is on a path to your own joy-filled life. That's what Trevor would've wanted for you.

To friends and family—I realize now that the years since Trevor's death have been difficult for you too. I can only say that I have a much better perspective now on what you may have been going through in trying to offer support. Thank you for trying your best to be there for me.

To Dylan, Kendra, and Annika—I only wish I could have made these last 5 years better for you. You are all amazing people and I look forward to seeing where your lives take you.

To Rob—I'm so blessed to have made it through this grief journey and find you still by my side. I believe our marriage is stronger for it.

To my editor, Nancy—I appreciate your kind and gentle support to help me get through the self-publishing of my first book. I couldn't have asked for a better first editing experience!

To my fellow "Voxy Ladies" Rina, Cheryl, Carolyn, Yolanda, and Karim—without hearing your voices daily, this business-building and book-building journey would not be half as fun.

Thanks for all your encouragement along the way. You have become an important part of my life.

Nina Nam—What an awesome accountability partner you have been while I've created and published my first book! Thanks for all the support and encouragement . . . now it's your turn to hit "Publish" . . .

In remembrance of Nina Powell: Nina, I will always remember the support and guidance you gave while we were on the author journey together to get our first books published. I'm sad that you aren't here to celebrate with me, and that we never got the chance to celebrate your book. You will always be in my thoughts as you were an integral part in helping me create this book that is going to change so many lives. Thank you.

To my fellow authors in the SPS Facebook Group—your support has been amazing. When I needed inspiration, I always knew I could reach out to you. I hope I can be as supportive to you when you publish your books.

THE **"SHATTERED BOOK COMPANION JOURNAL"** is available to download and is a continuation for those who are interested in doing more personal work for themselves based on some of the concepts mentioned in the book.

The companion is a short 13 pages, but comes with encouragement and questions to ask yourself so you can start living with greater clarity, purpose and happiness.

Head on over to www.rebeccatervo.com/index.php/companion-journal/ to download the FREE Companion Journal.

Please Help—

THANK YOU FOR downloading my book! I really appreciate your feedback, and would love to hear what you think.

I read all reviews and feedback I receive.

Please leave me a helpful REVIEW on Amazon by following these instructions:

1. Find my book by going to http://a.co/egiuaRn or by typing "Shattered Rebecca Tervo" in the amazon.com search bar.
2. Click "customer reviews" next to the 5 yellow stars near the top of the book page
3. Click on the box that says "write a customer review"

Thanks so much!

Rebecca Tervo

ABOUT THE AUTHOR

R EBECCA LIVES IN Negaunee, Michigan, with her
husband Rob, daughter Annika, and dog Teddy. She has a
passion for reading books and doing self-development
work. She loves to spend time with Rob at country concerts
and Packers' football games. During the summer you'll find
her on the beaches of Lake Superior. She loves to travel with
her family to amusement parks where she is just a little too
scared to ride the biggest roller coasters.

Rebecca spent over 20 years as a CPA working as an auditor,
cost accountant, QuickBooks consultant, and director of
finance at various companies. She wrote a QuickBooks guide
for small businesses that she self-published and sold to clients
on her website in 2010.

With the launch of this book, she is changing her focus to help
women overcome their life obstacles to live the lives they truly
want. If you are interested in learning more about Rebecca's
coaching services, please visit: www.rebeccatervo.com. Also
you can email her at rebecca@rebeccatervo.com or send her a
message via her Facebook page at rebeccalynntervo.

SELF-PUBLISHING
SCHOOL

NOW IT'S YOUR TURN

**Discover the EXACT 3-step blueprint you need
to become a bestselling author in 3 months.**

Self-Publishing School helped me, and now I want
them to help you with this FREE WEBINAR!

Even if you're busy, bad at writing, or don't know where to start,
you CAN write a bestseller and build your best life.

With tools and experience across a variety of niches and professions, Self-
Publishing School is the <u>only</u> resource
you need to take your book to the finish line!

DON'T WAIT

Watch this FREE WEBINAR now, and
Say "YES" to becoming a bestseller:

Go to http://bit.ly/2pxP3uo to Access the Webinar

Made in the
USA
Middletown, DE